OMNESIA

[ALTERNATIVE TEXT]

W.N. Herbert is a highly versatile poet who writes both in English and Scots. Born in Dundee, he established his reputation with two English/Scots collections from Bloodaxe, *Forked Tongue* (1994) and *Cabaret McGonagall* (1996), followed by *The Laurelude* (1998), *The Big Bumper Book of Troy* (2002), *Bad Shaman Blues* (2006) and *Omnesia* (2013). He has also published a critical study, *To Circumjack MacDiarmid* (OUP, 1992). His practical guide *Writing Poetry* was published by Routledge in 2010. He co-edited *Strong Words: modern poets on modern poetry* (Bloodaxe Books, 2000) with Matthew Hollis, and Jade *Ladder: Contemporary Chinese Poetry* (Bloodaxe Books, 2012) with Yang Lian. Born in Dundee, he is Professor of Poetry and Creative Writing at Newcastle University and lives in a lighthouse overlooking the River Tyne at North Shields.

Twice shortlisted for the T.S. Eliot Prize, his collections have also been shortlisted for the Forward Prize, McVities Prize, Saltire Awards and Saltire Society Scottish Book of the Year Award. Four are Poetry Book Society Recommendations.

W.N. HERBERT

OMNESIA

(ALTERNATIVE TEXT)

BLOODAXE BOOKS

ISBN: 978 1 85224 962 5 *Omnesia* alternative text
       978 1 85224 969 4 *Omnesia* remix

First published 2013 by
Bloodaxe Books Ltd,
Highgreen,
Tarset,
Northumberland NE48 1RP.

www.bloodaxebooks.com
For further information about Bloodaxe titles
please visit our website or write to
the above address for a catalogue.

Supported by
**ARTS COUNCIL
ENGLAND**

Cover design: Neil Astley & Pamela Robertson-Pearce.

Printed in Great Britain by
Bell & Bain Limited, Glasgow, Scotland.

In Memoriam
Maxamed Xaashi Dhamac 'Gaarriye'

(1949-2012)

CONTENTS

PREFACE

Dear reader, I apologise for the position I've put you in. Not just you, but the bookseller, the reviewer, and the various assessors through whose hands one or both aspects of this book has or have had to or will pass or passed – and indeed my publisher, who painstakingly produced two mirror versions of it, one of which you are, probably with increasing reluctance, reading now. And to what end?

Our culture is as happily full of mash-ups, remixes, and directors' cuts, as it is of variorum editions of novelists, poets and playwrights. It is entirely possible in the world of e- (and p-) publishing to imagine any book having several versions, supplemented by additional materials through websites or pamphlets. So, I wondered, why not write a book which absorbs that flexibility into its basic structure?

Hence *Omnesia*, a book in two volumes and neither, its title both a portmanteau and a sort of oxymoron, pairing 'omniscience' ('You must know everything') with 'amnesia', an often traumatic condition of forgetfulness. For me, writing a book of poetry is both of these, simultaneously a shoring up and a letting go. (In fact, for me, being in the world is also like this – perhaps that's why so much of this book is on the move, between tones and genres as much as places, not quite at home in any of them.)

So writing a book of poetry becomes both punk experiment and prog system. That is, I go with the emphatic flow of its inspirations, I forget everything a poem 'should' be, and improvise its subjects, its themes, its forms and tones, but at the same time I am constantly trying to orchestrate these into a whole, thinking of them as sections that contrast, complement and speak to each other.

This echoes my reading experience, in which any book that has moved, troubled or changed me begins to exist as one version in my head, and another in my hand. To the extent to which it has such an effect, it becomes 'my' book, and begins to be imagined as a collaboration between myself and the author, or by a sort of third mind that knows what we both know. Then, when I re-read the actual book, I find there is so much I have forgotten, or overlooked, or mistaken, that it has become yet another book. These two versions then enter into further dialogue.

While I was writing *Omnesia* – or rather while I was lying on a bed daydreaming before an event at the Cuírt Festival in Galway – I began to wonder if these various dynamics could be embodied in two physically distinct but twin-like books.

In my first Bloodaxe volume, *Forked Tongue*, I had suggested the principle of 'And not Or' to position a poetic of variousness in a market that favours (if not fetishises) concision and restraint. All my books since have been doubled – linguistically, stylistically or thematically. *Omnesia* takes that principle one step further: the various sections in each volume mirror, juxtapose, continue or contrast. Hopefully, they make one sense read in isolation, and a further read together.

What this interrelation does not appear to be is a dialectic – it is not that debate between thesis and antithesis which our media loves, creating pantomime oppositions in order to pitch common sense against complexity. It's more like the dance between ideas we encounter in the ancient mode of strophe and antistrophe, each step taking the step it echoes and reflecting it onto another level: the epode arises from this, not as a matter of logical synthesis, but as news from nowhere.

Of course, you needn't concern yourself with this unless it engages you: this volume can be read by itself, and only if you are at all moved, troubled or changed need it be considered in conjunction with its non-identical twin. I hope you are (moved, troubled or changed), not least because it will double my sales, a consideration I should confess occurred to me almost immediately after the principles outlined above.

Would you believe it, Ariadne? The Minotaur scarcely defended himself.

JORGE LUIS BORGES, 'The House of Asterion'

The whole is the false.

ADORNO, *Minima Moralia*

Omnesia

I left my bunnet on a train
Glenmorangie upon the plane,
I dropped my notebook down a drain;
I failed to try or to explain,
I lost my gang but kept your chain –
say, shall these summers come again,
Omnesia?
You'd like to think it's God that sees ya
(while He's painting the parrots of Polynesia)
give your wife that fragrant freesia
and not the eye of Blind Omnesia.

I scrabbled here and scribbled there –
a sphere of peers declined to care;
I roomed with hibernating bears
and roamed where cartoon beagles dare:
protect me by not being there,
Our Lady of Congealed Despair,
Omnesia!
You'd like the universe to please ya,
your admin duties to be easier,
instead you grip the pole that's greasier –
the shinbone of unskinned Omnesia.

I wibbled there and wobbled here,
forgot the thousandth name of beer;
I filled my head with clashing gears
and tried to live in other years;
I passed on fame, selected fear,
watered your name with 'Poor Bill' tears,
Omnesia...
So you lack ambition and pelf don't tease ya?
still, me-memed mugwump prats police ya,
and Brit-farce forces queue to seize ya
for the purloined pearls of Aunt Omnesia.

I'd like to think the Muse remembers –
not that teaching starts in late September –
but the first of fire's dying embers,
that glow on Cleopatra's members;
my further lovers' choric timbres...
Did I fiddle with their numbers,
                    Omnesia?
You hope it isn't Fate who knees ya,
the Ship of Fools which makes you queasier,
or Mister Scythey come to ease ya
                into the arms of Dame Omnesia.

1 THE SOUTH

Who looks out with my eyes?

RUMI

Rumi Barks

Not five years since meeting with Coleman B
Rumi's translator in the coffee shop at Fourways,
and the café is gone, the father-in-law is dead

who set up it and the night-drive round Athens, GA,
to see the dark houses of REM – even the band, run off
like a three-legged dog – even Vic Chesnutt,

dead now as the famous are dead: found in others'
dreams like Mister Barks', back in Jittery Joe's,
the all-night hangout dry and cool, a palate

built out of outsized browning autumn leaves
as though it is already round midnight when he tells
the dream of the master already gone

who advises he begin translating but it's not
translation, the heart re-writes its own book, as if
seen over the page in a still-deeper dream,

as though a dog heard barking at the rim
of waking in a far part of town where the trains
groan, trundle and clank by for chained-up hours

inside the small hours beyond the yard you saw
lined with discarded ventilation tubes of long
aluminium, battered like giant worm armour.

You want to get up, to walk the cool grid
of streets until you know the breed, the face,
the almost-name the dog is barking but

you stay, roll over and return to the book,
to the puzzle of letters swarming away
always to the corners of the page, the way

the coffee cup haunts us like a Bauhaus
in the dark, white bone block outside whichever
window, a white tower till the lights go on.

I wake up to its thick white halo between my teeth,
a porcelain frisbee I fetched in my sleep
as though I tried swallowing the toilet again.

I follow its bluish round like a morning moon,
a water-tower no one else in the car can see
too low, too full of night-rain to clear the rooftops.

I look into it like it's a trumpet bowl
and hear its caffeine sing work on, beyond
your age; work: be saint and be not-sane.

I put it to my lips and whisper hush
across the crema, sip: no hellhound crime
has been committed here, no need to run.

Black Walnut

...he never had the sense of home so much as when he felt that he was going there. It was only when he got there that his homelessness began.
THOMAS WOLFE

No tanglewood to strangle these young shoots –
black walnut lines their drive. No loon-eyed looks
from greased-out gable windows. Koi-stocked pool,
a cruise deck porch, and rocking chairs
that horses could relax in, swag-crammed rooms
to hibernate the better sort of bears.

No TB-rattled brass beds like Ma Wolfe's,
the balconies glazed in and cheaply roofed,
her narrow pine board extra wing the proof
that ends would never meet. A flood of guests
flushed out her youngest's home into a novel
and turned his feet to never finding rest.

These two had built their business on a whim –
the realtor who took them on a spin
just nine hours from their bakery to theme
their lives around black walnut – what for him
was talking mountain air and drinking wine
for her was dressers, auctions in her dreams,
black walnut's haven haunting her designs.

The novelist returned and left and died.
Now guides keep all his rootlessness inside
his drunken father's books while they deride
the Radisson, a coffin made of glass,
that overlooks their dwarfish palisade
of letters, and tells us how this too must pass.

And in Black Walnut's hall, the guest-house-proud
told how she stepped into a fragrant cloud
upon the stairs, a ghostly cook's fresh shroud
of chocolate, and how the letter A
(though only in a photograph) appeared
upon our bedroom wall, then on a grave

not far from where, brain-fevered, he was dropped
into the rootless, peopled earth. She stopped,
but let her alphabet continue, looped
through all our driving and our flying home:
black walnut for the shade by which we're duped,
and scent of chocolate to disguise our tomb.

Looking Glass Falls

1

The Blueridge Highway blocked, not by late snow
or floods as much as fear of legal suits
arising from some trick of slush or ice,

we go by Hendersonville's little cross
of ancient-waitressed diner, hardware store
still selling steel-framed sleds, the cinema

with one-seat paybooth perched out front, a van
unloading Samuel Smith's, an English beer,
to waterfall-filled, Cherokee-less hills.

Then, by the roadside, broader than this byway
pretending like a rabbit that it has
somewhere much better it could go, the Falls:

Alice's head bowed so her glassy hair
streams down, rock shouldering or sheltering
above her, unsure whether it is wing

or cloud, the way the dream makes you unsure
of everything except itself, which we accept,
clambering unquestioningly down among

its pools, we let skin feel what eyes knew first,
dipping a foot so mind and body gasp,
agreed it's not a dream, or else not ours.

2

Nothing is being shattered here again
and yet again, we stumble to reflect:
although the sky and tall pine canopy

lie broken into pools, they are not felled,
and water, emptying itself, still fills
according to the weather, not the myth.

That head will never rise, we'll never see
those changeless faces of the young, the dead
outside the dream, and yet we still believe –

it is the animal and not the man
who has to dream, and hibernates beneath
our reasons for this outing to the woods.

3

We're strolling through those trees through which, signs say,
a bear might stroll, then rear, or lumber fast,
if we should meet a bear – more likely him

it seems, than those whose woods these used to be,
or who we like to think belonged to them,
and to the mica littered underfoot,

sharp glassy flakes strewn everywhere there's firs
as though a great lake, mirror to the stars,
a tribe of water, had been shattered here

and, farther west, casinoed into further
glitterings – dimes, chips, nickels – all of which
reflect the liberty of our approach

to the translucent pigtail of another fall
that's gnawing out a palate for its cave,
old column, cold bole, which we three embrace.

4

As Carroll saw, it is the first solution:
the glass between us must become a liquid,
a lake, upheld, a walk-in puddle, font

ninety degrees off gee. Both *l'origine*
and *le termine du monde*, as Cocteau knew,
face of the oracle beyond our fingers'

keyless print, upright mere, both grille and gate,
admitting nothing but the voiceless dead,
an anti-radio absorbing song.

To pass through the glass would be
to wear its engravings on your face and chest,
to insert the slivers in your eyes and heart

that stated you had gone beyond
all tenderness and memory, you had
become a Kay, KOd by nothingness.

   5

The third fall's an organic waterpark:
hundreds of metres of chutes, pools ground out
by the broad arse of braying, flailing glass,

a sloping saddle worn away by years
of travelling that never had to leave –
the Trail of Tears as metamorphosis,

turning from turtle back to frat-boys' slide,
though winter's turned its tap to trickle now –
it's like a pelvis threaded by a worm.

The tepid sunlight keeps both cafe and
its treaty of cold beer at bay till ice
unplugs itself, dissolves its grip on likeness,

admitting tourists with their urgent throats
like hollow pilgrims to admire themselves
as tumblers, fish that call and birds that swim.

6

Why was the mirror shattered? Not to make
us animals again, blind to the shapes
our outsides carve, since we long ago reserved

our innerness as self. Without a cause
beyond its own fragility, it frames –
since we can never be restrained, retrained

so we don't start to read – how we observe
the frailty of icons to the self,
our whole face broken down into its tears.

Compelled to glimpse, we spy another force:
scattered in fragments through the empty woods
and at the feet of waterfalls, we find

ourselves rebuilding that which never was
intact, as though we thereby joined its tribe,
that shield which all the legends neatly fill.

As though each glint could be translated by
those dumb interpreters, the eyes, into
lucidities the light does not possess.

Dream Ironing

Side 1
Like waking from some symbol-heavy dream
to the shaving mirror's fog, your crumpled face,
you must re-iron out the crazy pleats
of ancient T-shirts of a Saturday

and listen to the sequencers on *Encore*
ripple across whole sides of vinyl – still live
in the US in 77 – which sat
upon the shamefully-untrendy shelf

through house-share years, while you consider how
cotton, which has a memory but no will,
will keep those creases years of casualness
have folded over hems and under sleeves.

Side 2
Just as your weaknesses survived Punk's dream –
you think synthetically, in double albums –
obstinate cotton returns every time
to the folds the body taught it, not the iron;

remembers like a vengeful elephant
years of neglect as though in Mirrorland
it raised a foot above your head – how unlike
dear Peter Bauman, Edgar Froese, and Chris Franke

politely introducing themselves again
then reconstructing their acoustic ark
in plastic notes, steam-gothic as the spaceship
that we supposed our future had to board.

Side 3

To be upon another world must mean
its meteorology sounds Mellotronic;
its fields Farfisal as the thistledown –
sisal and flax blown round in synth-winds under

those bubbling ARP aurorae; dwellings vaguely
seen under Moogish swellings: so it was
for space rock's light decade, and so it is
für immer in the shimmer of progstalgia.

Cherokee Lane knows how we slink back in
the Monolight, Clearwater Canyon feels
our worn-out trainers' tread: that other world
is where we lapse into the Desert Dream.

Side 4

And cotton, shall we claim it cannot think?
Given inhabitation of such length
as weskits know in Dickens, how do we judge
its readiness to find old fault lines?

It understands although we think we know
how everything must change as though we were
the stoic engineers of betterment
and loss, we also feel somehow exempt –

we're the recording, not the scratchy vinyl,
or the performance, not the ageing ear:
cotton recalls the link between our habits
and habiliments, and wakes us from the dream.

Pilgrim Street

*Having recently travelled to many new countries, through different
settings and places consecrated by history and poetry; having felt that
the phenomena of nature and their attendant sights did not pass
before my eyes as pointless images…*

LISZT on 'Les Années de Pelerinage'

1 *Chield*

My voice went on a quest to find itself –
it never breathed a word to me about
its divvy divagations. On the shelf
I fashioned fonts from flies, their snorkel pouts
for punctuation, trumpet crossed with trout.
Meanwhile, its palate for a scallop, off
my voice went down to Pilgrim Street, to shouts
of dry support from beetles, left one cough
to build a colophon: my capitals
were spiders and my type trepanned through ancient skulls.

Hit that bone ceiling and both past and future
glaze over, right and wrong brick up, the floor's
a stairwell with no spine. So Jung's computer,
which consciousness can access with a snore,
hovered in darkness like a bat indoors,
mute, while, monkey-mouthed, my voice immersed
itself in others' words like lakes; explored
each continent in haste for signs of verse;
sought out new Helicons of alcohol,
new mountains for old muses and new ways to fall.

So for these last few years (let's call it seven,
since numbers please compulsives and the page),
I've been invited on my travels; even,
(let's talk it up) to make Geek Pilgrimage.
A very passive knight, I must engage
with other peoples and their poetries;

must leave my house and, almost, act my age –
that's me, for whom 'outside' is a disease,
whose verse is manga made iconostasis,
obliged to learn, to taste and visit actual places.

Of course (I know this now the ship has sailed),
the whole clan was nomadic way back when –
before we built our boat of fools, fools trailed
from Africa – plus proto-Herbert men.
Yes, long before the reed became the pen
we all went walk-n-wadeabout who crossed
to Yemen when the Red Sea was a fen,
spread from Djibouti to points north. We lost
some melanin like luggage in the Ice Age,
then claimed we were sole authors of the human message.

We feel the same about our prosody
today and, whether we must innovate
linguistically or craft our monodies
on Morgan or Donaghy, we think we're GRRREAT...
Forgive me if I drift from that debate
back to my sad *otaku* quest: the game
of justifying what my instincts state:
the Silk Road and the Low Road are the same.
(In Japanese *shūgyō* means errantry –
while here it means that Shug disputes yir parentry.)

The Low Road and the Silk Road are the same:
you needn't know yourself to cross the globe,
and no cartography's required to dream,
but still, the Gobi's twinned with frontal lobes –
your neurons are oases; myelin robes
protect their merchandise of messages –
neuroses must be sold to allophobes,
philosophies spice up *la grande sagesse.*
My ancestors, though never so far east,
were travellers, twisters, tinks, skeletal at thought's feast.

The Herberts tend to yield sarcastic chields:
travelling showmen, shooting gallery
and shoggie-boat proprietors – from fields
of dupes drop to a lorry driver's salary –
unhappy scrappies, stickit merchants, at sea
in sober streets; quixotic engineers,
faith-loupers, seekers of higher calories;
genealogists of the tricky years,
brickies not thickies, dyers not liars: the cream
of chicken soup of those found drowning in their dreams.

Otaku: (Japanese) obsessive, geek.

2 THE MESSAGES

Established words also have their after-ripening.

WALTER BENJAMIN

The Messages

1

When Ally Bally Bee
fell doon the treacle well
he took a wee bawbee
to see what they would sell

soda farls for workin carles
pigs' lugs for their nurses
OVD for thee and me
GBH for purses

falafels for beginners
polystyrene stovies
goudie cheese for dinner
(Eh could eat a pair of rovies)

black puddin white puddin
puddin heid and red
a samplin of dumplin
beh a bigger bed.

2

The messages were written doon
in cuneiform on clay
back when Ur wiz hauf a toon
we aa began tae pay

Sumeria soon consumed mair
Salonika had sales
there's omega 3 in Linear B
two for one on Wales

thae Ides were gey untidy
back when Caesar took a faa
saying, 'Brutus, see's twa bridies
and an ingin ane an aa.'

hauf a peh fae Santa
nae caviar for Lent
there's the maik Eh'm aain ya
and noo meh loot is spent.

3

The message is that sassidges
are definitely the boys
while ham and eggs and wooden pegs
should not be used as toys

gae mental wi lentils
scell the frozen peas
there's mammon in salmon
and pints of ankle grease

there's sannies for trannies
grannies for sookers
there's chewny for loonies
and toes for veruccas

be human as the bakéd bean
and mad as six bananas
we still have jam for wir yestreens
and spam for wir mañanas.

4

The messages keep comin in
like dandruff fae the stars
the messages are drummin in
fae souks and fae pazaars

aa the fruits of progress
pantsuits for the ogress
DVDs of *Dangerman*
cardboard bottles plastic cans

everything organic
fresh fae the *Titanic*
there's nae praans in a Cullen Skink
nae calories in haen a think

Ally Bally all at sea
seekin oot his mammy's knee
hush noo bairnie dinna fret
ye can't aye waant the thing ye get.

The messages: shopping; *bawbee:* haepenny; *pigs' lugs:* pastries; *stovies:* potatoes
stewed with gravy; *rovies:* jute slippers; *beh:* buy; *gey:* very; *faa:* fall; *see's:* fetch
me; *bridies:* shortcrust pasty filled with mince; *ingin ane:* bridie filled with mince
and onion; *maik:* haepenny; *aain:* owing; *scell:* spill; *sannies:* sand-shoes, gym-
shoes; *'grannies for sookers':* Granny-sookers are a boiled mint sweet; *chewny:*
chewing gum; *yestreen:* last night; *praans:* prawns; *Cullen Skink:* a smoked
haddock soup; *haen:* having.

To Porridge

'Auld claes and parritch...'

Captain of oats, braw brose, fine gruel,
you are thi Scotsman's constant fuel
fae New Year's Dey till end o Yule
       (we don't do Simmer):
oan ilka morn ye bring renewal,
       thi stomach's zimmer.

Ye greet us lyk a fu-fissed mune
and guarantee tae fill wir spune
wi fushion – see, ye're cratert roond
       wi seas o bubbles –
tranquillity is aa yir tune,
       and ease fae troubles.

Grey revolutionary fur guts,
jump-starter fur thi slo-mo slutz
that sends us loupin fae wir cots
       intae wir sarks
(a dram in you gets slob and klutz
       back tae thir wark).

When snaa faas owre thi Border's pale
and Southron bairns can plunk aff skail
then even English journos hail
       wir Northern mannah –
are sudden experts oan oatmeal
       tapped wi a sultana.

Ye're like a clood-occludit sun
that casts grey licht oan ivrywun;
thi siller ash on grieshoch; grun
       ablow thi slush
that derns oat-germs that sune will wun
       thru Winter's crush.

Tho Doctir Johnson caaed ye food
fur foals – mair fulmar him – ye've plooed
thru Scotia's lard-imprisoned bluid
      and freed oor veins:
dae mealie puddins dae us good?
      Great Oat, explain!

Hoo dae we luve ye? Some wi cream,
wi hinny, spice or jeely reamed,
while Calvin's crew hae sauty dreams
      o fare of auld,
powred in a draaer fur bothy teams
      tae slice oot cauld.

'Auld claes an parritch' gaes thi creh
wance we hae drunk thi Daft Deys dreh
and neath a sober, saft grey skeh
      we view thi year –
we're nae whit bettir, but we'll treh
      wi sic guid gear!

Fushion: wholesomeness, strength; *slutz:* a leap in skating; *sark:* shirt; *grieshoch:* red-hot embers; *dern:* hide.

The Silvery Bridie

Twas in the year of 2011,
a date McGonagall will be eagerly marking in Heaven
(or, if he isn't there then in some nearby place
they put dead people when Peter can't remember your face)
where he'll be seeking whatever passes for parole
that he might walk amang us and read verses from a scroll,
that in that blazing core of Kulchur known only as 'Dundee'
famed far and wide unto the snide above and below the sea
as the hame of discerning columnists and delicious marmalades...
and also some ither thing that currently evades
my tiny brain, an architectural firm called Kengo Kuma
expended quantities of building *nous* and not a little *pneuma*
to design a Silvery Bridie to hing ootowre the Tay
and delight the porpoises and sparlings upon a summer day
(at least those who do not read *The Courier*, who might know to
        swim away),
and impersonate an aircraft carrier, though one that has no planes
though as neither of our new ones do, the result is much the same
as the Dowager Empress's great ship of marble, erected in Beihai
        Park
instead of paying for the Chinese navy, and all that offensive
        capability lark;
and all at the request of the Victoria and Albert Museum
tho our Empress and Prince Regent are never there, should you
        call to see them,
a situation McGonagall's dull shade knows anely too well
for they turned him awa from Balmoral as though he was a bad
        smell;
not that the V & A are offering to pit their paw in pooch
and pay up for the biggin, sae we'll aa be on the mooch –
perhaps it shall not happen, which may be just as well,
though surely then McGonagall will do bad deals in Hell
and sell the city's soul so that he be resurrected
and skelp the city's erse should this not be erected;
but may badness of all varieties flee far from our prospective
        Gallery

and may it lure an Englishman hence with sniffs of a respectable
        salary
to make up for the lines of Casuals from Whitfield and from Fintry
who'll suggest he take his building and insert it in anither kintry,
though I'm sure the Silvery Bridie will delight many a Dundonian
such as does not take a drink and sings to their harmonium
the civic psalms beloved by sic as love their municipality
for its bandstands and shrubberies and subliminal banalities
for here is where the couthy meets the *anime*, the wifie meets the geek
and where those internal aliens, the hip, meet for coffee in mid-week,
where our robo-zombie bardie hears a dictum he must stick to
as the Reverend Gilfillan cries, 'McGort! Klaatu barada nikto!'

An e-pistle (see opposite page):
Feardie: one easily alarmed; *darg:* work, a set task; *dree:* endure; *scrievin:* writing;
toom: empty.

An e-pistle

(to Stuart McHardie)

Aa hail thi hobo crehd McHardie
tho mair a feardie than a Yardie
and less a lairdie than a lardie
    ye fecht thi fecht
Eh hear there's some claim ye're a bardie –
    that canna be richt.

And noo ye're geean me a beckon
'Eh've written this – whit dae ye reckon?'
a sang aboot Midsimmer chickens
    or some sic trash
tae read's lyk crossin Corryvreckan –
    Eh'll hae a bash.

Jist send it herewards and Eh'll scan it
as tho it werr some bran new planet,
(Doc Finlay hud a fling wi Janet
    that soonds mair fun).
Eh've fingernails tae clip but, damn it,
    this maun be done!

Mind, things are no that braw wi me:
thi darg is mair nor maist can dree
an scrievin, aince a piece o pee,
    can find scant room;
while readers? Faur as Eh can see
    thi toon lehs toom.

We Scotsmen o a certain age
reside in a linguistic cage
that isnae what ye'd caa thi rage,
    pair avatars:
we'll hae tae turn ilk ither's page
    and shak thi bars!

Dichtung (Till Awa Wi It)

Thi message isnae information
thi wey a train is no thi station
        an a journey's no thi rail;
thi message huz nae destination
thi wey a voice is no narration
        an yir life is no a tale.
Thi message is an eisenin
   that cell speak unto cell;
that seabirds sing horizonin,
    that deean men maun tell.
        Thi message is aa presages
          o whit we waant tae mean,
        thi poem a golem
          that canna speak, jist dream.

That messages hae meanin – mair
than whit or hoo they mean: we care
        aboot thi guarantee.
Pit aa oor value in exchange,
feel thon philosopher is strange
        wha thinks there's mair tae pree.
But if message is economy
   wi nae ecology
then meaning lacks autonomy
   tae mak apology –
        a hammer tuke tae grammar
          wad niver cure thon greed,
        rebellin owre spellin
          is circuses, no breid.

Thi messages ur whit we gae
because we don't know whit tae say
          aboot thi fact we speak;
we tak oor crust and then we pay
and, payin, sell oorsels away
          since money's fur thi weak.
The message is that Capital
     usurps thi place o Leid:
we mean tae mean, perhaps, but fall
     tae meannesses insteid.
               Aa lenders ur defenders
                    o thi gruntin that is grift;
               aa debtors furgetters
                    that language is oor gift.

Eisenin: longing; *'Thi messages ur whit we gae':* to 'go the messages' is to go shopping; *leid:* language.

Lament

(for Harvey Holton)

Pair Harvey's deid that draftit *Finn*,
he's crossin owre thon drumlie linn
whaur naethin nesh can noo begin
    as green as grief
oor ranks are growein unca thin
    wi nae relief.

Thi hoonds that hunt, thi spear that slees,
thi stag that rears his heid then flees,
thi harp that sings o scenes lyk these,
    are been and gane:
noo he's been cairried on thi breeze
    they're scarts on stane.

Fae Corbie Hill across thi Tay
lyk wagtails wurds are blaan away
intil the Seedlies whaur there's nae
    lug they could catch;
ayont, Schiehallion's blankest page
    whaur nane will hatch.

Pair: poor; *linn:* stream; *nesh:* fresh and lively; *unca:* very; *scarts:* scratches;
Seedlies: the Sidlaws.

The Fogbow

Ghaist o a gaw that few hae seen
paintit on fog lyk a fugue o thi scheme
Noah supposit thi Lord tae mean
    when aa were drooned,
ither hauf o yin o His een
      thon runic roond.

Rope o smoke lyk a loop on a cable,
Grisaille Cain tae thi rainbow's Abel,
ultra-blank tae infra-sable,
    auld noose o tow;
Yin that's strang whaur Yang is faible:
    faur are ye now?

Gaw: bruise, rainbow; faible: feeble; faur: where.

Cock of the North

Did you furget that therr's a speirit in meh heid?
        Zat why ye dinnae ken we're speakin fur thi deid?
Wad you no notice gin yir lugs began tae bleed?
        Eh knelt doon beh thi quayside o thi Acheron,
puked meh innards upwards till Eh wiz unborn,
        Keelrow Charon graned but hud tae tak me oan
                coz Eh'm thi Cock o thi Deid
        frae thi Tyne up tae thi Tweed
        yeah Eh'm thi Cock o thi Leid
        (sae don't believe a wurd ye read).
Eh crossed thi Bordir wi thi Magpeh o thi Ninth –
        thon charm thi miners tint when Thatcher tuke hur tithe.

Jist keek doon thru thi hole that Eh shot thru meh foot
        and clock meh total lack or need o ony root
coz that's thi shaft up which thi messages aa scoot.
        Eh dipped meh tae and tongue intae thi River Styx
and fur nine year or mair meh heid wiz Weetabix
        but noo Eh dole out doldrums lyk Eh'm shittin bricks
                coz Eh'm thi Cock o thi North
        frae thi Tweed up tae thi Forth
        Yeah Eh'm thi Cock o thi Broth
        (aboot a leaky bowl's worth).
Meh heid's a cuttlebane, meh dick is Embra Rock,
        therr's budgies gnaain oan them gettin toxic shock.

Dye beh auld Saussure's idea that thi name's a bawd?
        He says ut disnae matter whit a thing is caad
as lang's it comes when it is telt tae, lyk yowes and Maud.
        But baptised in thi Lethe Eh forgot tae swim
till God tuke ilka particle and caaed it Him –
tae list His ivry name creates him limb beh limb
                noo Eh'm thi Cock o thi Say
        frae thi Forth up tae thi Tay
        Yeah Eh'm thi Cock o thi Sway –
        Eh'll crowe upon yir dehin day.
Therr's a grouse that's stalkin me and singin rebel sangs
        But ye're welcome still tae jine us as Eh hirple alang.

Dye hear thi Sirens boomin oot thi ile is gone
        alang beh Oceanus til thi Phlegethon
that's brunt thi keel an deck that Eh wiz staundin on?
           Aa thi wax at aa thir manin ut flew oot meh lugs;
aa meh wurds and ony meanin baith went doon thi plug,
        meh mouth filled up wi midgies and wi chafin bugs
             coz Eh'm thi Cock o thi Lorn
        fae thi Tay up tae thi Don
        yeah Eh'm thi Cock o thi Yawn
        (that's why Eh passed oot oan yir lawn).
Therr's an osprey that they spreyed wi braw insecticide,
        wheniver Eh wauk up he's peckin at meh side.

Thi Parliament o Burds is meetin in meh skull
        thi Furst Meenister o Scoatlan issa herrin gull
and whit he cannae heckle he thinks unca dull.
        But meanwhile auld Cocytus is defrostin fast
sune thi Deil'll feel his heels and brak his permacast –
        whit's comin hame tae roost is hoo tae come in last
             coz Eh'm thi Cock o thi North
        frae thi Dee up til thi Firth
        yeah Eh'm thi Cock o thi Yirth –
        and in meh wing Eh cairry dearth.
Thi ghaists o seevun hunnert years hae spiled thir vote:
whit's written oan thi waatirs says yir banes won't float.

Zat: is that; *tint:* lost; *tae:* toe; *beh:* buy or by; *yowes:* ewes; *dehin:* dying; *hirple:* limp; *brunt:* burnt; *lorn:* desire; *yirth:* earth.

Sealscreed

Thi mune is risin rantie reid
abune thi auld sea waa
as tho it werr thi neb o a seal
   come at some lassie's caa –
come steam-an-snowkin fae thi deeps
   at some pair lassie's caa.

Uts screed o licht flochts on thi firth:
turn heelstergowdie tae
see whit thi lift prents wi a skiff –
   whit huz thi mune tae say?
But nicht's aa ink, sae aa it's dicht
   is *waly walaway*.

Rantie: blazing; *abune:* above; *neb:* nose; *snowkin:* sniffing curiously; *screed:* script; *heelstergowdie:* head over heels; *prents:* prints; *skiff:* a light brushing; *dicht:* wiped, written.

Stookie

There's a stookie oan meh ankul,
a stookie oan meh shin,
and a stookie oan meh shank'll
shairly keep me in.

Eh've a stookie oan meh hip-bane,
a stookie up meh back;
Eh've a stookie oan meh ribcage,
someone's plaistered up meh crack.

Eh've a stookie oan meh spaulder
sae Eh'm hunchit lyk Eh'm douce;
Eh've a stookie oan meh wristbane
sae there'll be nae mair abuse.

Yeah, ye'd bettir caa thi janitor,
thi doactir's haen a laugh:
therr's a stookie oan pentameter
thi length o a giraffe.

Eh've a stookie roond meh thrapple,
a stookie roond meh skull;
When Eh rax oot fur an apple
therr's a stookie oan free wull.

'Cause therr's a stookie oan meh drinkin,
a stookie roond this book;
therr's a stookie oan meh thinkin
because thi wey ut knits is crook.

Therr's a stookie roond oor world
lyk we trehd tae mend an egg,
but it's biled and then it's birled
and we've sooked oot aa thi dregs.

Therr's a stookie oan thi Deity
since He fell aff the cross –
He got plaistered beh thi laity
sae He'd ken wha wiz boss.

Therr's a stookie oan wir universe,
tho thi wound is oan the swell –
and tucked ablow, oor mooths aa pursed,
we're thi rumplefyke fae Hell!

Stookie: plaster cast; *spaulder:* shouldblade; *douce:* meek; *thrapple:* throat; *rax:*
reach; *bile:* boil; *birl:* spin; *rumplefyke:* an itch around the anus.

The Shapka Ultimatum

shapka or capka, capka or shapka,
shap shap shap
cap cap cap –
which one to wear today?

TRADITIONAL RUSSIAN SONG

When frost first gees yir fiss a slapka
Eh swap meh bunnet fur meh shapka
till fickle sunlicht springs its trapka
   and fur turns leid.
Sae – Russki lid or genteel capka?
   Ye'd need twa heids.

Thi shapka taks me back to where
meh heid wiz when Eh hud mair hair
nor sense; ut sits – hauf-debonair,
   hauf bearskin rug –
restores meh lang-lost fringe and, mair,
   ut hugs meh lugs.

A black cap marks full stoap tae Winter:
tho Boreas laives his ice-wurm blinter
doon ilka street, tho puddles splinter
   ablow wir feet,
there's keekin snawdraps – droukit hinters
   o an end tae sleet.

A bunnet is Spring's harbinger:
ut sais, whitiver blasts occur,
Eh daur tae wear bare ears – nae slur
   o bein feart
fur me! Eh am nae passenger
   in hail's hand-cairt.

But still, a shapka speaks o steppes
whaur Cossacks flex thir quadriceps
and Pushkin's ghaist or Johnny Depp
    maun drift, snaw-blind –
this nitherin, switherin time's precept?
    Be in twa minds!

Leid: lead; *blinter:* flicker of light; *droukit:* bedraggled; *feart:* afraid; *nitherin:* freezing; *switherin:* undecided.

End-Sang

Noo aa thi seas rin dreh, ma luve,
lyk seevin gantin whales,
and ilka feech-choakt thrapple's coughed
uts final scrip o sail:

Cresseid quos ane, and *crammasy*,
and *speshlz* croaks a third –
sae ilka sang Eh sung tae thee's
a threid o lang-droont wurds.

And noo thi rocks hae meltit back
lyk lips and lea nae bane,
thi sun's a rosie in thi dark
sae nane shall see tae sain:

Auld Reekie's graned, and *stretterhawl*,
anither crehs *Kilmeny* –
sae ilka sonnet's net's been trawled
fur oor leid's blude-reid penny.

And as thi ainguls fae thi lift
lyk ashy keys descend,
ae last commandment is oor gift:
lyk *pillie wantons*, end.

Gantin: yawning, gaping; *feech:* filth, miasma; *thrapple:* throat; *lea:* leave; *sain:* bless; *lift:* sky; *ae:* only one.

NOTE: the seven italicised words are from key Scottish poems by, in order, Henryson, MacDiarmid, Leonard, Fergusson, Morgan, Hogg and Dunbar.

Pilgrim Street

2 *Οὐδείς*

As is our wont I went wrong somewhere, lost
my bearings, drive and hair – and didn't care.
I lived among the anecdotalists,
the giant babies and the well-prepared –
those lappers-up of milk who never share,
those darlings who use talent like a fist.
Out cold so long I thought myself sleep's heir,
I haunted my ambition, some dumb ghost
persisting when its family has left
the building: like an old card stuck to a reused gift.

Part of the art of pilgrimage accounts
viz. Chaucer, Basho and Byron, is the way
that characters or people (these amount
to much the same from far enough away)
actually go to places – as you may
have noticed, in these stanzas journeying's
more meta- than it's geo-: mere display,
these off-Spenserians are travel bling;
Vuittons that voice while other poems look,
recitative within an operatic book.

What is it that these caravans convey
but choral commentary? That 'tell not show'
the orthodox can't bring themselves to say
nor radicals allow themselves to know.
What is the news from no one? Let it go:
your argument's with Yeats, not with the self;
art's brief, it's comprehension that's so slow.
Let others smash your vanity like Delft;
doubt ego into nothingness, confess
to everywhere and no one; neither blast nor bless.

Because the huge dumb effort made to master
everything shoved into my lines of sight,
scent, sound and touch, keeps flailing, I'm a plaster
of jade and jaded – played-out, over-bright.
Meanwhile my family of themes must fight
through jute and ice-floes, jumbling into gray –
plasticene's rainbow, porridge viewed at night –
my thankless crank invention kept from day
by those who play more focussed melodies:
ambition's route one dogmas sound great in journalese.

The contrast is Sibelius and Mahler:
the nation in a synaesthetic note,
then silence; or the symphony's mad sailor
who's fool enough to build a flooded boat
then let his leitmotifs escape its throat
in bubbles, doves and flotsam, unicorns
in bottles, crows – whatever stays afloat
till taste's neap-tide can toss it on its horns.
Time cuckolds both types with posterity
largesse won't second-guess nor will austerity.

The contrast is neat Chopin, lavish Liszt:
the quickie Minute Waltz or *Les Années
de Eurosprawled Pelerinage* – the quest
or the quintessence; 'little corpse' or 'play
it differently again, "threefold" Orphée'.
The contrast is kerygma or the Kirk:
how gnosis only knows what it can't say,
while dogma's only silence is the smirk.
But those who tucked Liszt's butts between their breasts
knew sometimes a cigar is... I forget the rest.

Travel beyond your reputation's pale,
that limited and limiting domain
where few lights blink at your departing sail
as concave as an eyelid. Dark explains
by swallowing your craft from aft to name:
Ulysses' only freedom was to pass
beyond the expectations of his fame
into a sea that shattered guilt like glass.
From 'Oὐδ' to 'εἰς' his conscience was released
to splice his vanity to pieces and to peace.

3   METANORTH

But we are not finished yet; we can go deeper. There is nothing to fear. Give me your hand, take another step: we are at the roots now, and at once everything becomes dark, spicy, and tangled like in the depth of a forest.

BRUNO SCHULZ, 'Spring'

For Bruno Schulz

I never meant to go there but I went
left at the Brandenburg Gate, pausing at
that undulating square where long black stones
without inscription plumb diverging depths.

And down the thousand lanes that criss-cross
these blank-faced benches, tombstones, monoliths,
the people drop away and reappear
as though the underworld could be appeased.

I'd sat in Hedwig's concrete dome an hour
above the U-bahn's ghost loop through the Ost,
not far from all the burning of the books
that would have – if they could've – featured yours.

You leave me in a church for long enough
and I will weep at the proximity
to comfort, always hovering even when,
apparently, the dove will not descend.

But lost within these polished roots of stone
where I will never have to meet your eye,
I feel I'm stepping in a doorless dream
where home, hotel and hospital are one:

your planet built anew from postage stamps,
on which your nesting father furls his wings;
his ledgers filled with earth and cinnamon,
our lives connecting by a paper hinge.

Two girls pop up between two nameless stones
as though from prone – and I remember how
Théâtre de Complicité staged all
your hairspring work between the trigger's pull

and when the Nazi's bullet left your brain –
you'd gone for bread and I had come back home
between misdiagnosis and the scan,
my skull endangered for a spell as yours.

That fictive act, my tumour, cracks its jaws
yet cannot swallow up your bullet's fact.
These stanzas rattle, cans or cars or casings:
neutral, they send all neurons down these lanes.

Some of us may not mean to but we play
at hide and seek with strangers here until
the distances between us make me smile –
you found such deeper canyons cut within.

The Ship of Łódź

Ex navicula navis

Kuchen and coffee-coloured saz sit in the shop windows
of the great street of Łódź
long keel of compromise laid down in cotton
beneath the canting city arms
by German, Jew and Pole
from the weavers of Silesia to
the Ghetto that clothed the Reich
but only wove its shroud and not a sail.
'Lose the legs to save the trunk,'
King Chaim tried.
'Give me your children,'
King Chaim cried.

Pork fat and violins in the ersatz restaurants.
Two statues sit on Ulica Piotrkowska:
the pianist smiling at his keys
in urbane bronze, the poet silent on a bench.
Rubinstein's nose is long-rubbed for luck,
Tuwim's bright as his Epiphany crown.
The lid of the grand's a frozen wing
beating Chopin's notes in history's face.
Pilot of a brazen ship,
poor Chaim lied.
Listen to the tremble in the tram-lines still:
everyone died.

NOTE: 'From a boat a ship': motto of Łódź.

The Glass Cathedral

So there was I in Hamar when the sun would never set
upon the glass cathedral, drinking a six-pack
of Ringnes and thinking how we hold
the wound intestines in our diaphragm's embrace
as though we were a soft clock. And there we were
down by the longest lake, Mjøsa, into which
the sun refused to skinny dip all night,
down among the rising green of fields, so green
it seemed all Norway was a giant's golf course,
the mown hay gathered in white plastic bales
like moon-droppings, *jotun*-gutties, swollen bones.
And there was the small cathedral, cloched in glass –
or rather a ruin, pent in its pyramidic wedge
because thin air would eat its stones,
its attempt at a unlapsed apse.

And everything we saw on that unending day
and therefore see now seemed set along
that half-gone nave – the feast of twenty-three
ranged from young to old along a white-napped table
lapped with waves of gravalax and midnight berries;
a little eskimo of ice-cream or its plastic sign
the sun pretended it would sink behind;
the drunk man puking in an undark doorway;
the parents patrolling in their luminescent shirts
as though there couldn't be enough light shed
on what we do like children, eagerly alive.

So this was visible night, *Glæsisvellir*, darkness unfallen,
St Lucy's opposite, bare as the mountain, all eyes' white –
it seemed as though so much time crowded into
the plug of now, it made a clear gel through which
no further tick could ever force a tock,
each synapse lapsed before its leap, each wristwatch
stopped in aspic, each death-watch in amber,
in the fallow forever hour in which we joked

of eidetic North, Jokkmokk, that furthest town
where half the year is dark, half light,
where we would take up residence inside
a colossal day, break our fast in January,
lunch throughout June, as though sat on a carousel
astraddle Mercury's griddle-girdle, turning from
the uttering void to vocal glare, as though we rode upon
great painted wooden snails or slow nomadic whales.

And all that nightless sleep I dreamt we were
worshippers in the glass cathedral, bowing to
a shaft of golden sand – no God but God
still took us in a speculative hand and shook
the temple till the granite turned to glass,
shook to see where all our psalms would fall.

Jotun-gutties (neol.): giant golf balls; *Glæsisvellir:* glittering plains, site of
Odainsaker, 'Deathless Acre'.

The Lake in Druskininkai

I fitted in a palm
and there was still room
so that I wouldn't fall out
I braced myself with my feet
sharp as buckwheat

DAIVA ČEPAUSKAITĖ

1

The straight road and its forest's flanks
recede into a saltire; the fourth triangle, sky,
lightens toward the vanishing point.
   Totem poles in pairs

stand carved half-Christian and half-not
with virgins, suns, unsaintly souls – the old wood greys
where it isn't painted; a damp-eared fox
   lollops across the lanes.

Two-tone bark on the tall fir trunks
is umber dark below and russet raw above
the heads of the oaks caught turning orange;
   birches pass in batches;

The deer upon the roadsigns rears
and seems to hike beside us on his hind legs like
the shaman startled in the Lascaux caves –
   he is a stag with palms.

2

All the little languages must huddle by the lake
I told myself at 3 a.m., misleading a reluctant troupe
with tales of how dissident poets would recite
from a floating platform while flaming pedalos
bore them to and from the shore's applause.

The trees tried upstaging diurnal statuary –
that pantheon along its paths and the colossus
of Gandolfini in his dressing gown, columnar legs
piercing and supporting a pizza parlour – how could
streetlights' nerve-ends, branch-cradled, compete?

At this hour that ragged electric halo could barely
slink between the drizzle, so only a seep of city
illumined the mist-worms, lugubrious upon
the lake's brim, which reimagined my reflection
as Grendel looking up, unable to name his twin.

I was the afterwards he knew to be a myth.
Murderousness slept like toads in the mud
beneath him, at the entrance to the other world.
While he gripped the lake in a blank amplexus,
we lost each other's voices in the dark.

3

It's very rare that you encounter
in the hour before dawn or rationality
a blue wooden church shuddering so that
its bell-shaped teeth tintinnabulate,
but here it was, confessing. We drew near:

What must it matter or to you
that things, undemonstrative or
undemonised, may happen

to be translated for a while
into a form of speaking
we cannot take as scripture?

Without the great man's death
the opposition of forest to a lake
is only tonally an elegy.

Where there is no winter of warm coitus
discovering a lovelessness of voice
will never stir Erato's readership.

Without the tanks upon the boulevards
that poetry sales and troop levels fall together
altogether lacks an epic sting.

What is the matter with the matter
of Europe that a balance sheet should fit it
better than bedclothes or a shroud?

4

Only very drunk people were with me by this point,
but I wasn't one of them. I was filled with serenity,
as though the universe was vibrating, but I
was still. I reached for my camera but it felt like
it was miles away, as though there was a lake
in my pocket and a forest in my fingers.
I reached down through the freezing water.

Helsinki Syndrome

'Tervemenoa, Sankarimatkailija!'

1

Try to hear Sibelius's immolated last symphony
to this swoop across a vast flatness just
emerging from the shrink of mercury globules
from sea to inlet to lake, each reflected blue
as though a strange thermometer was shattered by
some immanence of snow and silence.

Listen to its charred Eighthness while driving past
seaweedy green and orange trees; instead
of hills, great outcrops of granitic rock:
erratics and moraines in the melody that leads
beneath the city's massive drooping eaves,
stormproof tenements and matt black cupolas.

Night's turning everything to glass
in the deco centre, as though allowing ice
to enter and to coat the Lasipalatsi and the Rex,
the toothpaste-bright neon sign for POSTI opposite
though at the station still thickset statues hold
twin winter suns against the midnight's gasp.

2

Think of the meta-north as a Glenn Gould thing:
a switched-off morning fountain where four seals
spray a daringly bare-nippled nymph
with Scotland's same gray-green old water
that chops around the sheltering peninsulae
where Rennie Mack's at liberty at last to build.

Porridge for a rooftop breakfast; stroll by
a publishers' old scent of spines; new kitsch –
Cortinas on cards, dolls balding into trolls;
remember late-night advice on aquavit
from well-pierced barmen: already Meg and I
are seeking out the myth of lunch,

stomach as time-traveller back through
the symphony of sympathetic courses,
histories braised till inarticulate, the mouth
a dragoman of fables – translating last night's
reindeer carpaccio upon glass plates,
its cloudberry cocktail and elk steak into...

Ghost Lemons

(after a still life by Nils Schillmark)

thin as pith
without zest
pressed to the front of the picture
pale as mis-
shapen eggs
ready to crack with the craquelure

the plate
so friable a
raised voice or pale wooden blind
would shatter
its terrible hush
its glazed and shallow peace of mind

the knife
could not cut
even the shadow of this apparition
so it lies
like the doubt
that would trouble some chalk equation

two lemons
divorced
from any memory of curd,
sea-monsters'
corneas
long ago pickled and jarred

Helsinki Syndrome

3

We curl up like bark around the *Jugend* root
of a basement restaurant in Katajannoka,
dark-panelled like the forest gathered round,
elbow-deep in freshly-fallen linen, and compare
the Lutheran, white upon its placid step-pyramid,
with the Ouspensky Cathedral and its igneous perch.

Why do we care that one is Wee Free bare,
blond; much-handled pews with little doors
to shut you in with prayer, with Melanchthon
your marble stand-in for a real evangelist?
Or that the other stuffs its onion with boiled loops
of Church Slavonic, soapy icons, off-hand crossings?

Is it because the coffee is so good, the waiter
so precise, the dining room so small,
that everything is simplified to simile:
the Protestant salt in the buttery mash,
the herring in its oatmeal *oklad*, both are tonic
to Scots – we have to like the likeness.

4

There's something in us must succumb to silence –
each has their own, the way at Ainola
Sibelius took thirty years to fill its every room
with hush, replacing each note with its colour.
Synaesthesia in winter like a disorder of the sinuses,
the green-tiled oven was F major roaring in the forest.

Only the kitchen keeps its tune of ticks and drips
as though firs crowded in to hear him burn
that symphony which no one else could hear –
much like MacDiarmid tried on Whalsay,
Mature Art a fireball grabbed by Valda, unwound,
then never set aside and never done.

Resemblances are like what lakes make of us,
they test how well we tell that we are other
to ourselves. The cream suit hangs beside his bed,
crumpled by the ghosts of all his younger selves
into a pelt of chorus, a freezing cloud of song,
a blankness never to be worn again.

Pilgrim Street

3 *Icarious*

How many lives divide in three like mine?
Winging it, my trajectory got broken
Apollo-Houston-problem style, the line
went down for years of drift, till I'm rewoken
from stasis for a new career as token
creative in a school of brittle stiffs.
But for the first part, how it seemed unspoken:
literature, love, and love of Italy, gifts
that meant the Grand Tour should have been resumed
upon re-entry to a small Venetian room.

Mosquitos whined like my old nightly rages,
the canaletto echoed my retreat:
I'd be the father, figuring his wages,
who holidays in post-ambitious Crete,
Chania, where on a still-Venetian street,
coiling between an icon – Agios Giorgios –
and Casa di Pietro's stairwell peek
at Artemis in marble – fake, but gorgeous –
like Actaeon on ouzo, I ask the saint
how long you last with dragons gnawing at your paint?

While in that middle stretch, those seven years
of beautiful myopia that filled
with monsters far less frightening than peers,
it felt like we, gone wrong, were being filmed:
as partners parted, beds skewed, psyches spilled,
this was a movie no one else could see –
the same one Tzanes caught in oil, his still
in which God's hand commands the kill, and we
observe St George's armoured arm obey;
the snake head pinned, the globe-arsed horse half-turned away.

Old paintings like to bother me: one crude
scene nags, as though pile-driven down dream-deep:
white penitents process in pointy hoods
across the dark canals as though asleep;
crocodile through back *calles*, try to keep
out of the city's knowing drench of light.
I used to line up empties like glass sheep,
and mock my dog-like thirst – old appetite –
by popping done crisp packets on their heads –
numb echo of that dumbed repentance of the dead.

That dunce-self I'd escaped, or so I thought,
into the hides of books, still stares back through
the pages of their print-smeared *capirote*,
it gets by on my pride in what I do –
that sound between the truth and sounding true
which Guston's stubbly Klansmen (Nixons, hoods,
lynch parties lunked in lethargy) all knew:
most artists would look pretty in good in snoods –
the mirror in their heads, not on the wall,
tells them it's better to be nobody at all.

I tried to be the Sci-Fi afterlife
of presbyters, the whisper of a Pict;
the baddest of mock poets north of Fife,
a shaman (also bad), a Dardan sect;
one of the cybernetically Elect,
a surgeon (mad), a Lakeside idiot,
several horses; first Herebericht,
then Wedderburn – two priests within one Prod.
Somewhere between my ego and this verse,
Nobody has usurped my tiny universe.

Nobody is the lens through which we glimpse
the Cyclops' eyeball skewered on a caber –
that whale harpooned by five translucent shrimps,
great Duellist nicked by gnat-cloud, clutching sabre.

Nobody is the giant's ideal neighbour –
silver banana medallist, mere sub:
a great man only names his greater faber
when laurel-strewn or eyeless in the pub.
Do you aspire to rank nonentity?
Then join our club: a crew that never goes to sea.

4   MUQAM

In Memoriam Emran Salahi
(1946-2006)

What profits it to kiss a friend's face
And at the same time to take leave of him?

SA'DI

Sonnet

(for Emran)

How unlike memory you are, a shape
that folds both friend and fortnight into a phrase –
you feel like recognition, like the skull
of a buried horse, how it distends our own
into a resonance we can't quite hear,
a strumming of the nerves upon the bone,
distilling collisions within the word. Now you
are dead, I read my small anxieties
as premonitory, though they were all for me –
new notebooks, taking nothing I could lose
in plane wrecks I'd count down escapes from till
a return I'd not confirm a meeting past.
It seems you are the filament, dear ghost,
unwound across that deeper gap than sleep.

The Black Hotel

Only the best insomniac hotels have these
black marble halls in which all
the lifts can only descend,
rooms like the pans in a watercolour palette,
washed to a different depth of night
by some suicidal eight year old.

Heated floor tiles release another's aftershave,
the safe can't recall your code but is portable,
the slippers are skinned from the fluffiest fish;
hangers receive faint echoes from spatulas in
the five sleepless subterranean kitchens,
or from the motorcyclist revving around the inside
of the sluggishly revolving rooftop restaurant.

Your body lies like a plastic kit
in the cardboard bed, sectioned and attached
to a tubular frame of days.
Your viscera have been replaced by a steel
and concrete *Vampyroteuthis infernalis*
which has wrapped itself around
your blind cetacean skeleton
and these are both upended as

the earth upends itself, rolling into a dent in space
possibly caused by the devil's elbow,
rattling and settling with that bone vibrato note
till you become the façade
of Hotel Shimiánzhèng herself,
a black dragon doorframe, dusty as wood ear mushroom
with a black chanterelle for a trumpet;

till you become Sleeplessness herself,
a creature like a hillside with chambers in
its liver-smooth flesh, maintained by brilliant parasites.
It dines on rocks, finds statuary delectable.

There are galleries in its expansive gut:
you can watch their limbs and faces be digested
on Hotel Channel 9.

Your lungs are libraries,
the books are spiracles, fungal –
they stink like truffles...

Summer Palace

1

It's not a gauntlet before the gate
but an expandable bracelet of watch sellers cornering
you with all their fake faces set
as though to this quasi-nineteenth-century morning,

where a guide in full powerless servant costume
yawns in the roundel entrance at all tours,
and another in surgical mask takes a broom
to the defensive mythical creatures.

A woman drops sliced beef from her sandwich
onto her boot, picks it up without breaking stride,
and eats, much as the lake has been eaten by the smutch
of smog and haze, and is gradually regurgitated

as we pass through the Long Corridor's continuous
swirling current of cameras
filling Facing-the-Seagull Boat
and Fish-and-Algae Pavilions with false sunlight.

I see the last gecko of the season crawl
along a painted beam beneath Longevity Hill
upon which, like Lamia, Madame White Snake
must kill her husband with the shock

of her true nature
revealed by a pan-gnostic prat. Here
she's a pretty head on serpent coils
like an energy saving bulb or spring-heeled Jill

who has to travel as we will soon
to the Kunlun mountains for the mushroom,
Ganoderma lucidum, which resurrects Xu Xian –
a thing we never saw or knew we'd want.

We contemplate instead the stone
cold Boat of Purity and Ease
its marble engine lacking grease
to take us anywhere outside a poem.

And this is where we float to on that joke
the Empress played upon her admirals,
their funds blown in the fiction of its smoke –
there's something trapped in those unturning paddles that's running
       still.

2

I end up sitting on the little outcrop you reach
across a causeway by the Wenchang Tower
looking at man-made Nanhu Island and the hill.

A woman nibbles uncooked corn from a cold cob
and feeds the fish. Her shopping bag has decided
to say 'Good days' as though it knows.

The fishes' flanks have two dark strips which sandwich
a white stripe – they make me think of
a fluid comb, a fir branch, and something else.

The fish can only think in Mandarin.
They know that every image has another
contained within it that we cannot access

as though our symbols were somehow asleep.
A butterfly just flew past, low over the lake,
heading for what the layout tells me must be North.

The Dowager of Don't

So here he comes, the whiny one, as stately as a gloat,
　　advancing like an icecube on the skids,
he's thrown out all the metres that don't float his poems' boat
　　like you'd throw out all the pans but keep the lids.
　　　　He's a twit, he's a git, and I don't like him a bit,
　　　　　　he's the empress of the emptiness within;
　　　　he's a tit, he's a nit, he's a clapped-out piece of shit,
　　　　　　the epitome of wittiness gone dim.

His photo's like a trophy wife, far younger than he looks,
　　and as soulful as a hull of null can glow;
his reputation's permutations aren't dependent on mere books
　　but the knowledge that he knows the folks to know.
　　　　He's a twat, he's a rat, and he's older than the hat
　　　　　　that Polonius employed to keep him dry
　　　　he's the plait upon a gnat, he's the skin from off the cat,
　　　　　　he's the sprat the other fish refuse to fry.

Pray hold your peace or hold your penis while your empress holds
　　　　his nose
　　for the whiff of different viewpoints makes him ill
and he's detected there's objectors to his holy lecture's pose
　　whom he'd marmelise if only mooks could kill,
　　　　but he's a whiz with the scissors and he's snippy at the biz
　　　　　　of excising the exciting trace of taste,
　　　　he throws a tizz worse than Liz, he's what righteous wrongness is,
　　　　　　and his cranium's a Poundless space of waste.

Listening to Beijing Zoo at Night

It releases many types of snore into the night air.
Similarly I have escaped from a four day conference
and am insomniac for beer, dragging
an unfortunately too-polite journalist down Xizhimenwai Dajie.
My ear is pressed to the ornate gate, I am resisting
the temptation to break in and buy the polar bears
a bottled beer, inseminate flamingos and bet on the zebras
with Sichuan Golden Monkeys.

When we finally left the hotel's vast compound
the pollution had smelt of cold fireworks;
Mang Ke yelled 'Soccolan!' as he passed with Duo Duo:
two silver Beatles with still dark brows.

We race past the Moscow Café where,
as small riposte to the Cultural Revolution,
a year's wages could be blown on cake –
if you could get back from the country. In the square
four lines of Mohican-feathered locals do a fan-dance
to ward off the third ugliest building in Beijing,
its three nubby towers resembling
the character for 'mountain' – 山 (*shān*)
bad *feng shui* not only since there used to be a lake here
but because we haven't seen a bar all block.

Wenyi hails a taxi back to the zoo and the Seasail
where you buy an six pack and you watch
Fifties movies, soundless, in which the strong-jawed male
of our species almost kisses
the maybe daughter of the perhaps benevolent general.
Their skin and eyes and long winter coats
are burnished by the monochrome
to horn and hoof and bone.

Wenyi writes down the characters for '44 Tenants'
and, even better, 'The Spring of a Small Town'. Yet again
I'm nostalgic for something I've never experienced.
It's what we didn't do, as I explain to my now wary
new best friend – that's what we remember best.
Two days ago, he tells me, a drunk attempted to hug
the panda Gu Gu, and was bitten on both legs.

All that night a succession of silent animals
poke their heads through my hotel room mirror
and contemplate me benignly – yak, giraffe, gazelle.
They all look as though they've been stuffed
some years before. Ah well, I tell myself,
I fought the panda and the panda won.

Karakoram

Poplars line the highway while it's flat.
Emran and I swop the names of birds:
parastu for sparrow, *kabootar* for dove,
he thinks that magpie may be *chelchela*.

The mud-brick walls have a melted look
as though they're made of dirty loaves.
Written on the back of the green taxi
in one small town: *Babyface*.

The old man in black on a black pony on
the highway empty except for him and us;
the second old man with a large scythe over
his shoulder in the sudden midst of a busy stretch.

A woman in a white headscarf whacks
the shoulder of her donkey as her cart approaches
the main road and as we pass
I see it wince. We begin to climb.

When the bus stops so we
can take photos, pee and puke,
I find a rounded green rock
half-buried by the roadside, football-big,

like a jade egg that would give birth
to the Seven Colour Mountains.
A man perches on a huge boulder
overlooking his sheep –

above the sheets of silver schist
and the bands of orange rising through reds
and the further snowlines that exhale
in slow slewing showers, the ink strokes

for seven falling-rising tones or eagles
overlook his sheep.
In the middle of this vastness
a bicycle leans upon on its little leg.

We park beside a shallow moss-edged pond
that wavelessly reflects the widest valley,
and as the pseudo-jade sellers sprint towards us
I think, 'as above, so above'. We begin to breathe

within a ring of unclimbed peaks,
as near their summits as their roots.
This eggwhite continent removes the top of its head
as though there was a passage through its thoughts.

Finally we reach the highest lake, the largest yurt,
the politest camel, the longest speech,
the most breathless dance, the paradise
with nowhere else to go to but down.

NOTE: *Parastu* (پرستو) is actually a swallow; *kabootar* (کبوتر) means pigeon;
chelchela (چلچله) is used interchangeably for *parastu*.

The Glacier

Scrambling among the hobo pebbles, pilgrim quartz,
we were speechless on the glacier's black back,
surfing its slowest wave, listening to its Xhosa click,
its rhotic grind, its kilometre throat's distracted rattle.

We'd diceboxed off the Karakoram highway up
a broadening valley between the Uyghur villages,
their pease pudding walls, their carved palace doors,
corncobs drying on their roofs like giant pollen.

The only oak in Xinjiang spread over twin pillars
of a little mosque, the hills behind like opened crab lungs,
their dead men's fingers giving way to vast flat walls –
children lay down to see stray poplars on their tops.

The one mine entrance was a cathedral gouge
in a cliff-face so tall it made it seem a mousehole.
Then finally, parked by the concrete yurts painted
with scenes out of the official past and walking

through the churr of magpies towards the first firs,
the first Swiss-eyed glimpse of gull-shouldered peaks,
breathless in the highland air as though we'd smoked
ourselves down to a quarter of our proper size;

there was a flight of steps up to a blind crest
you had to rest before, during, and at the climbing of –
and then it was before you, the blackberry tongue,
the exhausted shit lolly, the lava-stained granita.

It had something to tell us that we could only learn
by climbing on its dead whale belly and holding out
our mobile phones to record its auriculate melts.
There was a voice down in its rootlessness that knew

the root to all our travelling, the small dripping home
of our incomprehension. All our friends yelled at us,
and while their echoes put the eagles off their glide,
the glacier quietly carried on carrying us away.

The Autonomous Prefecture

Between the Down and Up Horse Drinks I believe
I am fine, advancing down a *báijiŭ* gauntlet
of smiling maidens, strumming gents, shot
after shining shot sopped up by slivered beef.

My notes on the recital of *Manas* include
lively sketches of my brother and sister bards
and though their hospitality requires us to be pissed or rude
it helps to choke the boiled horse down. I'm quite the card

for several soup-bowl toasts between the sheep skull
and the inch long loops of grassy entrail,
and even in the hot lens of the square
Shu Cai, Emran and myself are relatively upright for

the cheapie camera I later open in error
in the desert, so these ephemera
are increasingly coronaed in apocalyptic orange
as we saddle up for goat polo on the homeless stormy range.

But when they stop the bus and make us damage
a final tureen
I take six of the seven steps that Thor, green
with the breath of the Midgard Serpent, managed,

and wake up back in the Black Hotel,
my grave goods neatly arranged
around me. I try a shoeless walk down its strange
corridor to see if anyone is awake in Hell.

As Eliot so sweetly put it, 'Our Iranian poet
had to be carried out
and the Scotsman was waving
his hands without saying anything.'

And in that blankness we were indeed autonomous,
shaken from the concept of our bodies,
gone in the gallop of nerve against bone that roams
down this burning wire which still threads the days.

The Muqam for Emran Salahi

Emran we barely knew enough
of what we were saying to know each other
except as gestures we could translate as kindness
biscuits flavoured with pistachio
like the echoes of good jokes, nougats
you kept conjuring as we crossed the desert

we couldn't name the tamarisks,
the magpies or even the stones
that gathered in small sets to watch us pass
in our bouncing trucks except as gratitude
in toasts of tea or pomegranate
or in the embraces

in the drunken blazing square
when we sat at school desks for the show
in our white Bonanza hats of Kyrgyzstan
those six-soup-bowls-of-*báijiŭ* hats
from when we did our duty at the toastings
that held our heads on for the goat-tussling

as our horses changed beneath us into torches
hanging in between the stars,
then packs of yellowing dogs, soap
and sacks of whiskered corn husks – they kept
on changing, lighting up the paths
between oases for the dead

turning into ropes ribboned with falcons' carcasses,
venerable tins of meat recovered from polar trips,
blood coagulated in sawdust, in kasha, in sand;
forming servants that should have bowed in each chamber
of King Heart, and rushed to do his bidding, horses once more,
though playing tembors and made of leaves

and now our lower parts were marble veined with green
so men could hardly bear us down the corridors
to bed, and stowed us in old tombs,
beneath the dome designed to trap
the silence of all nightingales, among
the concubines in coffins wrapped in silk

while in the blinding oblong door
we saw our companions were afflicted in reverse,
their naked legs lumbered and splaying
beneath their terracotta torsos:
the poet who was too great to speak,
the critic too important to shut up;

the inheritor of a radical hairstyle,
the friend of someone someone had once heard of,
the frank speaker of other people's minds –
all tottered past in cartoon cavalcade
and left us to the peace
of our complete incomprehension

as though in a cabin of that prince's boat
surrounded by boats of courtesans
singing bright songs in this strange country:
lanterns in the darkness, foreign throats
from which Ibn Battuta heard a ghazal of Sa'di
passing on the river in that absolute good night.

Breakfast with the Generals

Better than watching the brave postmodern poets
bully some regionalists because
they'd only read Gorki and hadn't heard of Hikmet,
(never mind the verse forms they thus
preserved), was breakfast beneath the giant Mao
poem in Seal script, calligraphy of emperors,
our patron's wealth getting us onto
a restricted base despite
the security risk of our blatant hangovers.

Gun barrel boys, gloves on, replaced fermented
milk with weak tea as I poured honey on
deep-fried dough like *churros* in Madrid,
blinking very slowly, bowels clenched.
My palate's roof kept sticking
and the generals kept joking
about a literary ignorance that went unchallenged
miles from the equally un-
mentionable border with Kyrgyzstan.

The General Composes a Four-line Poem

There is no afterwards with war
the seed of one will dream
within the ceasefire of the other
while the weaker find their own extremes.

Hangover Tuesday

On Hangover Tuesday everyone assembles in the square
wearing the correct colour of baseball cap –
taupe for kidney pains, canary for jaundiced, rue-blue for heid nipping –
to celebrate the twentieth year of bad hangovers.
This doesn't include the seven years of blackouts,
who have to stand at the back in the gutters.
We advance towards our old school desks, politely reciting
'the mountains strum the sky's cloud strings
until the river runs with music's blood'.
Our heads are giant red jellyfish balloons afloat
at the regulation height of seven metres, as we are in fact
at the bottom of a completely dry ocean.
Our necks are yellow banners which state 'This person has fallen
off his horse and cannot eat intestines.'
At regular intervals we run eagerly up to the high podium
fronted by clammy middle-aged palm trees and poinsettia
all growing from pots which contain our livers and genitalia
(their roots grip us with the correct emasculating gesture,
white as the tubercules of virginal mares).
We make speeches extolling the virtues of cities
we have never visited, which nevertheless we woke up in
this morning. These are translated into the official language
of Hangover Tuesday by a tiny female speaker
planted in our right nipple. It tweaks when she speaks.
Then we direct our bottoms at the heavens and emit
a sparkling firework show and a single butterfly.
Shining ribbons whorl as they descend,
each weighed down by a braincell.
Our names are printed on red labels transliterated
into ancient characters as 'Kicks the dead dog,'
'Tussles with the former goat', and 'Eats lung-cheese.'
We then seize our three stringed banjo which we bought
while temporarily dead, and recite three thousand lines
of an epic about the passionate love of a donkey
for its reluctant owner. You must recite all three thousand
in a single breath without puking. It has a galloping rhythm
and a distinctive rhyme scheme we can't quite catch.

Taklamakan

Our path is lined by giant topiary teapots
and a green man playing his leaf komoza
in front of or possibly for his horse.
These go on for miles but no one seems
to notice. Red willow, camel thorn bush,
jiji grass, purple-topped tamarisk;
grey cranes in the shallows of the artificial lake,
the Kunlun range like a high cloud line.

In the middle of the desert a hoarding for
'The Pacific Advertising Company'.
Sand swirls up a column like a ghost car
doing endless handbrake turns.
Little conical sandheaps dot the gravel,
like the abandoned humps of escaping camels.

The orange-jacketed road-worker lies down
beside the road ignoring the rare batriarchans
and their brethren, the nearer mountains.
At one point the two parallel ranges
are briefly, simultaneously interrupted,
agreeing to dip towards or bow before
a farther pyramid which may be their king,
his white jade throne, or just another peak.

Emran gave out *sohan*, a pistachio
and cardamom toffee; Abdul broke up
and handed out frying pan-large *naan*. When we stopped
to pee on the rim of the desert I heard a cricket
in the cornfield. Kubin said it was called 'zhi liao'
which means 'she knows she will soon die'.

Ghost

(Variation on a theme by Matthew Sweeney)

The ghost which doesn't know its way but must get home
stumbles in the desert through the day
and searches through the passes in the dark.
It gathers pebbles into maps to guess at its passage
across the great steppe in winter.
It immerses itself in lakes to feel
what the birch roots feel, it sits
in the bodies of sheep and goats
whose blood can't halt the chill.
It travels from mosquito to mosquito in
the fat summer air,
it wraps itself up in fallen trees' bark
like the text in a rotten book.
It only knows North and consequently
may be travelling in the wrong direction for months.
Sometimes it thinks it recognises
a configuration of poplars
and a great dread descends.
It lies with the maggots and the excrement beneath
a row of toilet stalls in Knife City.
It remembers faces seen with no thought for
the last time. Memories are diminished
and must be counted out like beads:
the ratchet in the old woman's throat,
the smell of cheap newsprint in
a now nameless airport,
the hand nervously gathering a curtain,
the baby's black button blink.

Night Market

These fish have crossed the desert to be here –
belly-up, eyes still eager – and so have we;
so press among the Uyghur breaking fast
on long kebabs dry-spiced with smatterings
of paprika and push towards the pile
of pomegranates like a mud-brick wall
translated into juice carbuncles, ask
the man to turn his crushing wheel for glasses
that look like lamb's blood, taste of rust-edged roses.
The market glows with coal-flares, TVs show
imams and kung fu, skull-caps pass for skulls
clapped on the tops of turning heads like wheel hubs
as we disturb *naan* sellers, chicken choppers,
with our un-native faces' late-night shopping.
Myself and Yang Lian, both alien,
are equally remote from West Xinjiang
while Emran's instantly relaxing – here
as in Tehran, the Muslim night adheres
to gentler pulses we recover strolling
beneath dry balconies they will soon fell
in favour of the corporate eclipse
of concrete that surrounds this slow collapse
of strollers and their hopes to a midnight bulb,
the one teashop left open in the globe
where Abdul knows to rouse the owner from
his double *hajj*-earned slumbers. Empty room,
low-roofed, where we can be loquacious on
long-tabled platforms, thin cream cushions;
beneath the dusty beams and over tea –
black, hot – as endless as we'd like to be
ourselves, but we must break this moment up
like bread, not knowing as we drain our cups
how soon this quartet of our well-warmed breaths
will be abbreviated by a death.

Pilgrim Street

4 *Katabasics*

Off-centre in the centre of my life –
that's how it's always been: the ideals slip
away, the mastery will not arrive;
while habits fix, reforms refuse to grip.
A daoist vegetarian, too hip
to compromise the future with his vote;
a dope who, vindicated by the trip,
still couldn't tell the ocean from the boat,
got off his floating world, grew backwards to
the family as art, then failed to follow through.

Inventing the vocation in the Haugh,
that cross-roads where a B-road crossed the Urr,
rewired my brain into an anxious loch,
a broth of hypochondria, a blur
through which an ageing doctor wasn't sure
but thought she saw a tumour like a trout.
A night in hospital is not a cure
nor are two tests, then three more months of doubt
before the scan, but as the auld man laughed
at midnight in the worried ward, 'They'll wheech us aff

and cover us in concrete.' Nurses drew
a conference of curtains round his bed
and left us dreamless, lucid, hopeless, new,
in transit through the outlands of the dead.
Mature art meant the carapace was shed –
no aping others' genius, claiming *nous*
while acting like a faithless infant ned:
there was a child that stanzas wouldn't house
but I could hope to father; a career –
the teacher first learns how to leave the House of Fear.

Those nurses and our muses are the same:
they've dealt with us and with the likes of us
before, grand vanities and little shame –
sometimes vice versa, but, whatever, thus
it is with these vile bellies: just adjust
perspective on Parnassus, say the Nine,
and watch us go – first flesh, then rot, then dust;
they overlook the final twitch of lines,
footless as snakes who treat their tails as teats.
Go mouthy or go mute – you go, they wash your sheet.

When I was on the Low Road's darkest patch,
a baby girl upon my shoulders, the cats' eyes
that should have lit its single track all scratched
out by anxiety, I recognised
them as my ancestors', their colour prised
from black and white, my gran's old greeny blue
made cataracted marbles, and surmised
I must still be in hospital, not through
its lidless night, not yet, not waking up
for months, just learning where you go without a map.

When I was on the Silk Road's lowest stretch
between the two oases' green-tiled tombs,
Peach Blossom Paradise beyond our reach
behind the Kunlun's range of grim jade gums
all fanged with ice, our livers had no homes,
our hangovers were nomads and our lights
revolved within our bellies, since our bones
were swopped for sharp dust-devils – in that night
I saw the frightening place I'd visited
back in the Haugh, though like the country of the dead,

was never there at all, instead it was
a Helicon, that habitation next
to clarity, awake to lack of cause
and simple as cold water's lens, its flex
of sunlight in cupped palms. Placed outside text,

you watch that scorpion beside your foot
and see it has no goals, is unperplexed
and ready as a sickness. There's no route
that leads to anywhere but here; no shame,
no game: the Silk Road and the Low Road are the same.

5 LOWRY IN SHIELDS

[Lowry] is not making a social comment on man or his environment, but revealing a type of mental organisation which sees the world from the heightened standpoint of a watcher or spectator. Moreover, the spectator himself becomes identified with the scene he is watching; he is not only spectator, but is himself aware of being under observation.

NORMAN COLHOUN & HAROLD PALMER

'Do you think so, sir, do you really think so?'

LOWRY

Lowry in Shields

1

Seaburn sees no ships for solid hours.
Its sea chops serpentine and slate and meets
the sky's lowering of lichen and concrete
at just that time when the light is deadened.

The long grunting tide snuffles in the sand –
that or the wind makes the lampposts twitch
as though they caught a scent of old moons
out past the asteroids, those frozen globes

which see the sun as punctuation in negative,
mix metals in lugubrious pools
like stews of boiled-down behemoth, the stink
of dead things retrieved from the ocean floor.

Lead on his tongue as though he licked a church roof;
as though he took the coin from a corpse's eye
and pressed it to his palate; as though he ate
a poisoned chowder with a pewter spoon.

That cold sweat which appears on the back
after unaccustomed exercise, as he has to sit
before the eyes of others in the dining room
in the discoloured shirt he didn't mean to choose.

2

Not even knowing how little it is I know –
thoughts like feathers between myself and thought –
still the little red robot-head room on stilts

that stands upon Herd Groyne at South Shields
is the spirit of Lowry or some unit thereof
as measured out by an exacting Salford hand.

And at the auspicious hour for leaving, when
in January the fish-pink dawn slides its fins
down Vespasian and Trajan Streets;

or when evening bestrides Jarrow's heaven
like a denatured lobster, cloud-clawed
and crane-feelered, then the ghost of an optic,

an outsized eyeball, is crossing on the Ferry,
rolling on the deck like a gelid bowling jack,
a softened pearl in a shucked oystershell.

3

Lowry is travelling still farther north. Although
he pays annual tribute to the mouth of the Tyne,
to the long oil tanker waiting beyond the bar;
gives thanks for its metaphor of the idler, lying
on a wall smoking a cigarette – that cypher for the self –

he wants more: to see the bashed-in front bumper panel
of a gold Nissan Micra on the Broadway, running parallel
to the North Sea from Tynemouth on to Whitley Bay:
to know it's like the funeral mask of the Mycenaean king
who Schliemann claimed was murdered Agamemnon –

bearded, beaten flat into an owl-eyed Janus, his profiles
reversed, looking into the innards of time: *kairos* as
the bridge of a nose, hinge between the chimes at midnight,
between Kronos and chronology – to give thanks
for slippage, that dreaming smash, stramash and setting out.

The Blazing Grater, *or*,
The Olympic Torch Passes Through Tyneside
(A variation on 'The Blaydon Races')

I saw the Blazing Grater on the fifteenth day in June
two thousand Geordie years and twelve, on a summer's afternoon
the Metro ran to Whitley Bay, where the mad and caald go bathing
haway we went to St Mary's Light – that's where the torch was blazing.

Oh me lads, what is this light that's passing?
the miner's lamp that foond the seam or the little fame we're rationed?
Aal the lads and lasses there, with fish and fried potaters
Gaan by Spanish City just to see the Blazing Grater.

By the Priory at Tynemouth and the guiding lights at Shields
the Roman baths at Waalsend and the Rising Sun's bright fields
the runners bypassed Meadowell, told the shipyards 'smell you later'
the unpaid stewards lined the route to cheer the Blazing Grater.

Oh me lads, what is this light that's passing?
the spark that fired the Rocket or the North run oot of passion?
Aal the lads and lasses there, with ice cream in a wafer
Gaan by the aald Wills Factory to see the Blazing Grater.

By the hyame of Hughie Gallagher, Wor Jackie and of Shearer,
the temple called St James's Park – each year wor faith grows dearer,
the flame it ran doon Gray Street to the Baltic and the Sage
a Monument to hoo the Toon found culture aal the rage.

But oh me lads what is this light that's passing?
the rushlight lit at Jarrow or a Southron sporting fashion?
Aal the lads and lasses there with suncream on your faces
Would you rather gaan to London Toon or to the Blaydon Races?

While the rest of Britain was still living in a barn
Bede picked up the Gospels' torch and welded Lindisfarne
But the Grater skipped the Scotswood Road, and poverty and trouble –
it's looking like a monkey show performed inside a bubble.

Oh me lads, this light has left us stannin
I fear it is the sort of flame that passeth understannin
Aal the lads an lasses there, aal smiling in a crater,
just wave goodbye to cash for growth and to the Blazing Grater.

The Shave

How to re-enter the nineteenth century
with its better class of axe murderer,
its limitless supply of tubercular
courtesans, its autonomous moustaches:
pass through the cervix of a too-hot towel
folded and pressed to your flushing face,
the apparatus of the chair cranked back
like a car-seat in a suicidal layby.
Small panics soften as the lathering brush
approaches with its cool aquatic kiss,
a giant otter on the Tyne's soft bank.
You find there is still more to be relaxed,
vertebra by intercostal cog, your shoes
loll outwards as the blade – an eyebrow of steel,
the moon's regard – begins, as wielded by
this nun-battered Dublin Geordie lass who lifts
your jowls gently in the snow-lit morning
and strums upon the fretboard of your throat.
For this is where all opera takes root,
the pulse of your nostalgia for unlived-in
eras, that sin of breathing elsewhere than
this greedy moment's need to blame, *verismo*
is only conjured by proximity
to blood. All chatter falls like an old key falls
and cuts the slush, the orchestra of combs
and scissors seems to pause, to concentrate
on this small nearby risping shifting note
as though to cracklings in an infant's lung.
She is the diva of scrape, the *spinta* of slice,
her tessitura runs from jugular
to nostril till she smacks you back
into the day you'll haunt with alcohol
and soap, anachronistic neck,
shaven and shriven and white as a baton.

Shields Cyclist

The old man cycling in a neat blue jacket,
check shirt and tie, flat cap and clips –
his bike a black-framed ancient, basket-
hanging, chrome bell trilling –

brings a decade in his rust-free slipstream,
his air force posture, bowling club pin:
the hot street swithers in a tarmac dream,
slang-reviving, drought-dispelling;

till the lard breeze rises from the ship-shorn harbour,
charver's rations, gun-fodder grub,
and he shakes in the wake from a four-wheel Barbour,
discount logoing, gastro-pubbing.

The thread his wet-tyred wheel has sewn
between the streets will dry up soon.

Sklent

Sometimes, coming home to Shields,
I glance down Stephenson Street
toward its open view across the Tyne,
and a sudden tower blocks my eye, its windows
blind as termites, building under glass.

Sliding like a berg in parallel, it keeps pace
so when I turn right for my house,
Beacon Street's already stoppered up
until my doorstep shows the whole ship,
blue-funneled, bound for Norway.

Once in, the senses of the old word 'sklent'
stare at me from the dictionary, like faces
skelling from the photo of a Wallsend yard:
it means both sidling and the sidelong glance –
I recognise our angle to its wake.

Building a Horse

That clopping down the street I only heard
while trapping sun against our garden wall –
not so remarkable it couldn't be
a horse, but, as it passed by, nothing tall
enough to be a rider's head appeared.

Was this how Eohippus sounded when
rain filled his two-toed spoor like stirrup cups,
the small horse dancing in the face of dawn?

I went out to our gate and saw three things
in black and white, as though their confluence
could build the beast: a collie and its master
glancing back at the crow upon the fence,
its eye upon some passerby's old chips;

then, where they passed the steps down to the quay,
a plastic glass that, having clattered past
my house, now stuck here, blown against the kerb.
The others walked or flew away; I paused,
just to affirm its perfect mimicry.

Shoeless upon that path before all bridles,
how trippingly he'd come, no hiccups to
his progress here down millions of wild years.

Another couple stared, so I mock-frowned,
as though expecting someone – then, a flare
of breeze returned and my chimera reared
and backed away, then raised his head to stare
the seawalls and the far horizon down.

The Bad Dog

What does it think they are, the kindly cars,
to shoulder at their bumpers, bite their tyres,
force them to crawl down Tyne Street while it barks,
panicked as if some scent approached in darkness?

Every two weeks or so this mutt escapes
from our dear neighbours, scrotes and car-key scrapers
to the invasive vehicles of gentry –
No fishing? Lead the life belligerent.

Released, the tyke creates a line of turds
that flank our house, ellipses for the wordless,
mile-forts, each one perimetered by stencils,
those yellow warnings left in turn by councils.

Animal too, and speechless, how your fingers
know something – see how they mistake your doors,
trying your office key at home each night,
and blithely, come each day, the opposite.

The good dog tugs at indecision's leash,
knowing the ways you're set in, rank as flesh:
as though aware the lesson is too hard,
persisting, tenderly, beneath your guard.

Tynemouth Lodge

Sometimes I go to the tavern and get drunk.
What of it?'

NESIMI

1

Bars tend us in our brighter afternoons
toward the gentler tenses: conditionality,
subjunctivity, would reign within
their glasses' stains, so that it might
be possible to claim, if there could be a bar
where Lorne Greene drank, post-Battlestar,
a whole Bonanza shot – if these
could somehow have been filmed
within these Borders, in this North East –
then it would be here where the piano is
forever paused, the Cylons placed on charge,
beneath this rippling cream ceiling motif
not so unlike the way his hair was combed.

2

In fact no keyboard need be present, just
the suspension of its mammoth tooth-tonk
will suffice, any further note defeats
both memory and prediction of our tune.

In fact succession can find no hook here,
like the gecko's tickly foot, baffled by
some non-surface, some lack of wall,
the brim of things must suffice for now.

3

The soft stabilities of brass and glass
in late Saturday sunlight, unsure
if it's still summer, gloss on green leather,
wrought-iron table legs tucked under sight,
polite as beetles, suds amounting to
a glaucoma lens of foam, and the muted flame,

111

sun as haematite immersed in the alien finger-
length depth of the pint's remains.

Lorne must rejoin us, his stunted doubles, here,
and pay off all his gunless hands with ale:
all princes among men are here disinherited
of their kinricks; in fact are here defined
by abdication of any claim upon the future.

4

Lorne! Lorne of the sausage
they do not serve here at six o'clock
alongside the pork pies and many fatty nibbles;

Lorne of the flattened sausages of Scotland
as though the issue of a union between
minced meat and a carpet tile!

Lorne of the knitted sausage! Only here
in the debatable territories between North Shields
and Tynemouth do we approach

the hidden etymology of his name,
Lorne as desire beaten flat with a patterned hammer!

5

You're lulled by recumbent frosted curves,
hill-silhouettes rolling across the panes,
one Jane Russellesque boob of which seems
tattooed in drunk Cyrillic, this bar's good name
picked out in clear glass, subjected to
a backwards encryption which reveals beyond

as autumnal, each letter burning copper
as if through a map. Above them sit dark suns,
the off propeller blades of unrequired ventilation
(since no one within can either smoke or breathe):
surely this means you're no longer sitting here,
surely you have passed right through,

and rest within the bower of those boughs,
tricoloured into yellowed glade, glad shade
and fish-depth green, their tolerating sway,
like looking up at seaweed when you're drowned.

6

You've reached the point where each theme,
each mouthed approximation of your days,
those chapters you've inhabited like cotton,
becomes equally accessible, equally remote,
and at that moment, you are become robot,
mute, unnecessary and beyond all script,
you are no longer little nor a Joe, who,
according to the thinking of his genitals,
is perfectly attractive to the ladies.

7

You have become the last animal, the lost anomaly,
an apology for a noun, the verbs' anthology,
each thought its own tautology, each nerve
as an autonomy, you're less than an anatomy:

a machine that can't reset,
the beast that must forget –

although no Houhynym would know you and rejoice,
no cowboy Cheiron ever cite you as his boss,
you have become, to use the parlance of these parts,
a son of Adama, a half-life, a second Hoss.

Nocturne on Hudson Street

There's a hole in my neighbourhood
down which of late I cannot help but fall

ELBOW, The Seldom Seen Kid

What is it Hudson Street constructs from drink
taken, the half-six Saturday walk home?
A mussel back of cloud, half-open, shows
its gullet's sheeny blue to all and Autumn.
A bright star's pearl is either shifting gears
to land, or Venus marking how some breeze
that we can't feel shucks off her cloudy shell.

Whichever, this short, tatter-tarmacked lane,
half cut-through, half a Metro bridge, has dusk
engrained into the anti-climbing paint
that's soot-sluiced down one wall. A wash of grime
stubbles its textless arrow which points out
the yard behind those galvanised claw posts
where all car parts which failed us are compiled.

The street's a clause, and 'DIAL _ OTOR CO'
continues with the still-unfinished Home
for Younger Ne'er-Do-Wells, now crested by
a wave-roof from some drowning architect.
Its sentence lacks a grounding verb: one house
might tune its gravel-throated ecstasy
to the choiceless evolution of a child –

small exile from this moment who'd confer
citizenship on all, without your say
we'll have to judge the worth of things ourselves.
What do we have? A folded page marked 'RAWN'
and thrust into a wired-off fence. The wall
on which a fall of harling has revealed
this wood strut like a frescoed martyr's knee.

Spanish Battery

At the full moon when the cloud's jaw slackens,
a giant snails' road lies across the river,
and the benches sit as though they were coffins,
exhumed and recycled by this light,
each timber black against the ground-tooth waves.

A lone land-cruiser's household huddles in
their cribs, ignoring that full-throated shimmer,
how it paints their sheets as shrouds,
chucks their offsprings' withdrawn, bad-dream chins
with a changeling's gauging finger.

Name-plaques gleam in the unaccustoming glare
as though the benches wore sunglasses after dark,
and all night nothing stretches its arms along their shoulders,
watching nobody pace back and forth where
the silver cobbles of that causeway cross the Tyne.

The Horse

I feel like a horse...
IGGY POP

More like a whippet than a horse he rests
between his rockings for a century
as though ensuring that last child is dead.
The narrow years have led him here, to this
shop-window shared with ripped-out mantletrees:
a January steed in Howard Street,
breathless between a mirror and the pane.

As though released he's riderless tonight,
as if returning from a valley docked
of tail or mane, gutless, his saddle torn,
his crocodile lens scuffed, his ears flat back
and stirrups rusted, and the little bar
that held his munchkin-cantering in place
is gone, preventing the collectors' bids.

And so he stalls here, known to me, so that
I almost hear him whinny through the glass,
'Remember that hot lane in Venice and
the frame de Chirico confined me to?
That doorway you stooped into, stupefied
to find me in a hoofless *calle*? "What
is this?" you laughed, and recognised me there.

For each of us there is a portrait kept
apart from easy likeness – face or age
won't yield it – though the eye, burnt back into
its socket, knows at once. It's twenty years
since you stepped back onto that baking sheet,
that street of beaten gold, as though it was
an ice floe, and my postcard in your hand

is long since lost. Why do you think it is
we've never left the shadow of this shop?'

116

The River Vanishes

The fret lies on its back on the Tyne
like a sulking centipede made of wool
and will not answer to the name of Haar;
it sends its feelers down every chare, each lane

to baffle the wearers of shades in Shields:
the dull knocking of their colliding skulls
won't drown out the horn on the pier.

Boats call like the shofar announcing
the Festival of Fog, while birds and the bell
from South Shields town hall are made clear
as icecubes by not knowing where they are.

A ship of indeterminate greatness growls on by.
To be in the heart of haar is to be separate
from light but aware of it everywhere; to be
at the fringe of fret is to notice how cold pulses,

how it is clammy as far upriver as Wallsend
where the mist mitheringly removes
the upper floors of the two multistoreys.

Blossom merges with its impalpable ancestor.
The sun is made moon by fret, is made its only fruit.
The river vanishes, but holds the key to sea-fog's plot.
We are closer to each other than we can see.

Pilgrim Street

5 *No Man*

Who'd be their mirror's image? Occasional,
alarming, mute – that's how we seem to most
of our acquaintance: why should they recall
what we pronounce, portentous as a ghost?
Our prophecies go missing in the post,
between the pillar box and lobby mat
of vague regard most scribblings get lost,
we are that backwards music heard by bats:
nobody's blues. Ear to the looking glass
you might just hear your reputation marching past.

Nobody and their looking glass shall see
nothingness doubled and redoubling till
the eye is shot into infinity,
a voyaging with neither wind nor sail,
still incomplete between breath and the will.
You fog the glass and see a mariner
or seem to, nearing through that curving veil,
old Zeno's leagues of instants: who you were
or who you will be, you can't tell – now, tell a lie:
why won't you look that apparition in the eye?

Because a nobody's a type of sin
now fame's our virtue, failures are consoled
present indifference means you'll one day win –
outside your lifetime's park, with different goals.
But that's obscurity's excuse for rules,
which liberates both players and the game:
no echo here of regs that hobble fools;
no chants, no crowds, no stadia, no names.
No skills are needed on a pitch so small
where everyone's a ref and no one has a ball.

But every poet is a nobody
to most of those who say they like to read
and mean the simple dead, plus two or three
the press explain are in the perfect lead
to be the era's metonyms in deed
and hopefully in print. Biography's
the apophenic art, which tries to weed
significance from chance – most hear its plea,
and few prefer that coiled complexity
the symbol spins out of a truth to set it free.

For nobody's that constant, clued-in reader
who understands why you keep leaving time;
who's nodding while you mash Krautrock with lieder,
or follows why you fossick other climes –
not seeking the exotic or sublime,
only directions for that journey home
you've never quite completed here, a mime
who cannot leave their abstract booth, glass tomb
in a cathedral to that martyred sense
Saint Sound, an absence granted by the audience.

Embrace all second places, spurn the spoils
gnawed on by the slow to comprehend
they're just another generation's foil,
winners who fail to grasp you jump off-trend
fast – slip beside the point or, best, behind,
before your self-importance gets impaled
upon the limitations of our time;
stay half-rhyme fluid – what you lose on sales,
credit or credibility, you gain
in heartsick wanderings and the hubris to abstain.

Between the divas and dogmatics, I –
or someone sounding just like me – must go
to Sofia or Jerusalem, and try
translating tunes which Dante didn't know;
to Tomsk, Kashgar, Hargeisa, as the flow
decides – Caracas for the western arm:
fish out Khant ballads from beneath the snow,
hear Amanissa Hanim's Twelve Muqams,
a herder's *hees* in the airstrip's quickened dusk,
the song of *el caballo viejo*, thick with musk.

6 BALKANICS

Hey, green parrot!
Tell is how it is in Europe!
The Green parrot replies:
Man is not symmetrical.

SREČKO KOSOVEL

Hotel Velina

1

Wake to the myth of the swimmerless pool,
steam rising to blunt the surrounding firs,
while in its shaving mirror's blur,
your white squid shape completes
length after length in effortless jets.

Big as a neanderthal brain, cooled
and free at last, and trailing legs
like spinal nerves, it monologues
along its teenage flank in flushes, bruises,
spots and burns, healing and returning as

the sun rises higher, the day lapsing into
a colourless pause, until
a dirty cream wolf advances on the pool
as though it were wounded
and laps at its hot stock of sounds.

2

Bears place their black elbows between
the orange shanks of conifers and push;
a mammoth's forehead sweats in the grass;
the dog with human forehands barks,
affronted by your mute approach.

This is the unconsciousness dismissed
by butting the pillow slowly, till your neck
feels beaten by a rubber weight,
adrift between the lake-isles of the ideology,
this is your bestiary for the psyche.

Tar drips from the wristwatch, its
little eyeball blinks with dates, your towels have
honeycomb smears upon them.
An owl swivels as the seconds click,
the worm coils in the steam room.

3

All this will be collated in the dark
distended stomach of a sheep –
that *gaida* Petir Bonev played
eight years ago in Yuzhen Park
still shrill and lilting yesterday.

Herded into its padded inner pub
past ovine portraits, armoured and ruffed,
as you recite the good word 'light'
a powercut translates it into night,
and Sofia becomes a gut.

In the darkness you see the symbols spawn:
if a sheep is a fish and a herd is a shoal
then your luminous skull swims in the nightpool
with the cleansed spine of a beluga –
we are only resting in what we know.

Red Square Radio

(Radio Café, Novi Sad)

How I loved   my red square radio   the size and depth
and with the receptivity   of an ashtray   just too large
for seventies' jacket pockets   neither Levi nor Wrangler
just too heavy   to carry round   on its black wrist-strap
its small black tuning wheel   blind   to where it was
on the medium   or long wave band   its round brassy mesh
large enough   to micro-mark   the straining earlobe
into which was inserted   frazzled blab   the hot zabba
of Beefheart's peeled   blues   his backwards desert bop
the Geiger knock   and fizzled calm   of radioactive rabotniks
from Dusseldorf   a transistorised chorba   of Albanian pops
Croatian crackles   sine waves of Serbia   mumbled news-
casts of Macedonia   and once   who knows why
calm cold tones   of the Galloway clock   the hours of which
fit exactly into   Krasnaya ploshchad   as though Malevich
were calling me   as though an icon   were a bell

Melodiya Rakia

Pear and orange and peach and grape,
apricot, melon and plum –
you can drink a rainbow, drink a rainbow,
then be boneless and numb.

The Brown Danube

On a floating platform being dragged
by a small reluctant boat
to a well-churched town, the name of which
I forget each time I'm told it
rows of chairs are set out beneath
an awning and the blinding Serbian blue

as though this were a little theatre set adrift
or a cinema only showing one film:
'The River' – broad, brown,
endless and actorless, so
my fellow audience members leap up, snap,
attempt to fill the frame.

In the brow-prinkling, nose-pinking light
I watch the constant wooded banks
be punctuated here and there
by a half-sunk, slime-streaked dash
of rowboat, then a parting in the trees,
then a grey hem of pebbles.

Within the dark green shadow
there's a pale green hut and,
in front of this sufficiency,
a fisherman plays himself as
Expressionless Man with Bucket,
looking directly into the lens.

Hotel Vojvodina

I watched myself attempt to sleep,
head and body in one sheet;
night filled a pit with shutting bars
where still, till two, they played guitars.

Between the hour the woman wailed
and when the bells for mass were tolled,
like Lazarus insomniac,
I watched my coiling shrouded back.

The bed a coffin, room a grave –
how often has this game been played?
To be the soul, let flesh decay
until commanded back in clay.

Beneath what pressure do we split?
When lust's illusions call for it:
those destinies that stand in doors
of heretics whose wives are whores.

Insomniac as Lazarus
till cleaners water-cannoned dust,
I rose and looked into the square,
but couldn't see who called me there.

Fly Novitiate

Large, bejewelled, and, for the moment, drowsy
as the libido of a forgiven nun, the fly
attached herself to my jacket like a mike,
a sick brooch, a vagrant Hitler tache

outside the white walls of Manastir Grgeteg,
one quarter of its courtyard carpeted
in onions, and clung to me for the stroll
back down a newly-funded gravel path,

between the mosaics of well-armed angels
and past the booth of bottled peaches,
pear rakia, and honeycombs floating in jars
like fragments of the Bee Cross.

Although I had to leave she would not leave me,
stepping around a brush from the back
of my hand as though I was just sweeping up,
and my jacket was a rug beneath her feet.

What did her buzz-purr expect? That we
would set up home together as man and fly
in that sag-beamed farmhouse on the slope
opposite, encroached by Fruska Gora's oaks?

That I would sacrifice that solitary cow
to feed our baby-faced maggot young?
But she had no goals, like an old woman
munching in a nursing home, no memories

of the desire of the bride for the bridegroom.
She could neither stay with me nor go
to shelter beneath the glass sword of Theodor Tyron
whose crispy relics lay in Novo Hopovo.

And I, abruptly tired as a fish who realises
it has spent its whole life swimming away,
got on the bus to go to the radio tower, the burst seedpod
of its bombed-out globe, and left her at the gate.

The Babies

I'm driving at night through the countryside
trying to decide what it is the countryside is
to the side of. Since we all already share
a perfectly good roadside – perhaps it's beside
this. Certainly there is more to it than verge:
it also has an underneath of sexton beetle,
a canopy of bat and owl and, by the sea,
another side, although, for some reason,
I can't remember which sea. In fact,
for the moment, I can't remember which country.
It's far too dark to confirm any of this
on this particular road, which is narrow,
mountainous, meandering between villages
without lights, banked by mounds of bushes
merged with eucalypti, beneath a milky ribbon
of stars. Then, caught in my headlights,
are two babies standing in their nappies, talking.
They are at once by the roadside and in
the countryside. One turns to watch me, thin-
lipped, drilling his eyes into my tail-lights,
the back of my darkened head, until
the car is out of sight. Then they return
to their sullen, unhurried symposium, as though
I'd never passed, as though I'd never been born.

Hotel Illyria

Suffled how it gush from the source of the woods of Tepelena
Motto on a bottle of Albanian mineral water

1

On top of the Venetian Tower
the horses Anna Comnena claimed
could gallop four abreast along
the eleventh century walls
have left their shoes nailed up
into the shape of the word 'Welcome'.

We drink chilled red wine outside
Durres's deserted bars, staring at
the black rubber sheet of night,
listening to the wash of the Adriatic
as the midnight ferry's lights approach
their memory of an horizon.

In the morning the sea has thrown up
a harvest of furry beige pebbles:
camel hairballs, kiwi fruits de mer;
the gonads of ague-cheeked dogs
or belching bears, snipped off by crabs
as a toll for the Brindisi crossing.

2

Sing, Comnena, all things round or rounding,
on or up, rolling, rotating or revolving:
Greek amphitheatre, Roman rotunda,
Byzantine cradling wall, Venetian torre,
Hoxha's concrete blister bunkers.

Simple melatonin tells us this:
there's a sun that, turning within,
will baffle dream. But years must creep
out of sync with mirrors, feet
find themselves in other zones

still not at home, before we suspect
heart's galaxy – *die nebensonnen*
round which our several selves
still orbit, turning maladies into
multiheliotropic hymns.

3

The slightly higher fedoras of Durres
are designed to let the air of Albania
rattle around like an unemployed bullet;
to let the hairstyles of Albania relax
between the fingers of the muezzin's cries.

They are higher than movie homburgs,
than the trilby of the mobster in the clipping
tucked into my soon-to-be-lost notebook,
who was shot in the hatband and said,
'I didn't see nuthin.'

In the square down from the mosque
the old men sit in their fedoras' shade and stare.
At every public bin
a little old woman
is assessing its contents with care.

Photos of death notices
are plastered to the lampposts all around
giving us the self-same look:
they want to know why we might think
we will depart Illyria.

4

Mistress of the untuned guitar
from whom the stars all keep their distance,
the sea walls and 'Pink Floyd' bar
have both agreed that there can be no resistance.

Gun-room both rounded and domed,
acoustically primed for war's song,
great Tower of the Venetians, condone
her madrigal, maddened, bedraggled and wrong.

5

the peculiar caffeine- and raki-inflected acoustic
if I can become a cucumber or a devil
of the cannon room in the Venetian tower
poetry sounds more beautiful from the legs of a woman
allows for flintlock whispers to become
Mr Casimir proclaims there is no death
artillery reports, insouciant announcements
I like my concept of trees more than my concept of concepts
to seem like mumbling confession
my penis doesn't like me
until it is clear that it is no longer clear
as Mr Sausage says, 'Barbarogenius'!
whether we are hearing poems
that sentiment was as cold as jam
or the thoughts of people who have to listen to poems
and now the real last poem from Mr Zeno

6

the dust on a fedora
a photo of the dust on a fedora
the dust on a photo of a fedora

7

On the bus to Berat's high backwoods
I'm wakened by a pothole's prompt
into pilgrimage, having dreamt
of the chicken backwards.

In the dream I was on the same bus
looking at the same Balkan estates,
their tractors' dismantled apparatus
their haystacks like stranded yetis

and I saw a cockerel with its brain
in its arse, its head empty as
a clean cloaca, retreating across
the fertile Albanian plain.

I watch as hens advance on grubs, tilt
combs at grit, and do not reflect
on history's direction
one little bit. I think of kilts

and kilters, heading for where
Byron watched the soldiers dance
and dreamt himself into Illyric romance,
heard North in a southerly air.

8

Lord Byron loved the Albanese
and geed thir wee white kilt tae Greece
tae clad thir sodgery and please
       Athenian lasses,
sae he could dream o Hielan knees
       and Morven passes.

Chield Geordie, lyk yir Duke Orsino,
thocht music wiz baith fruit and vino
tae thae wha loved, lyk Tarantino,
       the dream o war –
tho Mars wad shrug and read his *Beano*,
       and Venus snore.

Vyronos garbed lyk a Grecian ghillie's
mair like Malvolio than Achilles
at Missolonghi, mad and ill as
       the marsh is deep
till death made him a glorious *miles*,
       and let him sleep.

Hielan: Highland; *rowed:* enveloped.

9

Everything round or rounding,
on or up, rolling, rotating or revolving,
Greek amphitheatre, Roman rotunda,
Byzantine cradling wall, Venetian torre,
Hoxha's concrete blister bunkers.

The tiny chalky snailshells
we gathered, lying in the grass
before the giant head of Konstantini
i Madh, that keep falling out
of my breast pocket.

The town inside the castle walls
above Berat, its streets coiled
round the icons of Onufri,
a board that shows the monyplies
of unfallen Constantinople.

The number 6 of rolled-up meat
inside a battered schnitzel –
stinky cheese as though Cleo-
patra, forgotten in her carpet,
dissolved across the centuries.

Then the clouds gathered in
and spoke to us in Turkish
about *şimşek*, the suddenness
of light, and the way that sound
can roll across a valley, *gümbürtu*.

10

In the revolving bar above Tirana
we raise our spinning bottles to young Byron.
I toast the way he saw at twenty-one
his own sins living in an old man's skin:

two hundred years ago in Tepelena,
great Ali Pasha's palace in a glen,
he crossed 'Chimera's Alps' with Morven's Highlands
while that tyrant praised his noble little hands –

and so do we. I put my bag upon
the tower's unmoving shelf, so while we clown
my notebook becomes our satellite,
a little moon of text illuminated by

its twin's more distant eye, its graphite craters
filled with Scots' linguistic ghosts. Chimeric creatures –
midge-queens, gull messengers – devolute
my script: I'm Balkanised at forty-eight.

Elma's on cocktails, Arjen drinks raki,
the boulevards blink up: they're spun askew,
fleabites in negative. Here's a tiny world,
as true to us as he was to Childe Harold.

The moon observes the poem as zoetrope,
eclipsed by my high hand, its dizzy grip,
but loses our descent to unsteady streets,
our barbarous yet not indecent glee.

Thessalonika Is Burning

I wake to the smell of burning car tyres
in the broad bay of the hotel room.
Everything seems furred by lateness
as though it is that hour which lies between
the hairs of a sweating horse: the hour of beige.
The last thing I remember is a Slav cornfield
in blond and white, two horsemen who discuss
something the subtitles keep covering up
(from Russian into English under Greek)
about hordes and dethronements,
as though the fields burned around them.
As though the bedrooms burn about me
I pad down the corridor, feet bare
as if prepared for coals in the hour
of scarlet carpets, of the slumber of fire
extinguishers: perhaps the hellish smell
is in their dream. At the stairwell I tap one
like the cool chiming of a clock, then go
back to my room, alarmed as though I know
the biography of fire, how it visits this city
like a vizier in disgrace, a new Greek prince,
a Nazi with a list that just lacks names,
centuries of names. I gauge the smell:
stench or imperceptible? Something I trod in
or something burning in my head, the way
that at the hour of the panting shoe
every sickness could be with you, ranked
like the dead in your empty wardrobe.
I go to the balcony, to see where the fire is –
perhaps everywhere is burning, and only this
white tower is saved, sunk in the open mud
of the harbour. I look along the lanes of the road:
two lips of a mouth that goes on being shut.
Then as, still more nose than eyes, I blink,
like the last two people in a bar linking up,
two cars decide to crash beneath my room.

Their echoless crumpling crunch disturbs no one,
not even the drivers, who just sit there,
till the vanished sound is the same as the smell.

Quince in the Plaka

Να σκασουν οι εχθροί μας!

At table below the inscribed names of poets, which trouble
our Latinate eyes, we slowly translate their slogan as
'May our enemies burst!' I stuff myself among
their friends and an actress who tells McGough
his name is Roger Garfitt, and he is her old friend.

Near the Tower of the Winds, cog-octagon which ought
to spin, driven by its carvings' stubby wings,
the horse-fathering Anemoi, I sit next to
a lecturer who dives for shells year in and out
off the same island, and wears their spirals cut across:

their nacreous layers exposed like ruined stairwells
to the comments of the air. I'm offered quince soaked
in rosewater – a December treat: fibrous, cordial,
sweet like a scallop's sweet; Athenian yet Aztec:
the slices lie there, bled, surgical, sloped.

I taste a different winter, a muted Yule, luke-
warm: the emphasis elsewhere in this birthplace of
so many gods; the flavour's soft as stew, sea and fruit
combined, the perfume long, a rose reduced
to evening – it's like nosing the nape of my wife.

Let that scribbled claw of curses go burst
the bubbles of some elsewhere egos: I'll eat the quince,
as it becomes the baby heart of an Eastern Christ.
I never understood Him as bread but I begin
to digest Him here as samphire, mussel, quince.

A Few Days in Athens

I'd lost my watch by four: before I'd bought
my absent wife's Metaxa or the grain
of rice on which a woman wrote the name
Isobel. The Acropolis was shut.
The strap was faulty. Many shops sold post-
cards claiming ancient couples matched the films
the hotel wanted me to watch: hot thrust
for pay-view thrust.
                    Today the churches fill
with candles swaying as their bases set,
with people swaying as the chant melts in.
Today a visit to the Parthenon
is free. The winter sun is still so hot
it dries the sweat my back brewed on the climb
to sit above the city, out of time.

Kolonaki Square

What does that little chorus sing,
the canary in a cage outside the Café
Bibliothiki, beside the British Council,
that placates the restless customers within?

Because our ears are too slow for its song
I must approach instead the bronze
that echoes the exterior of Elytis
and lives like he did on Lycabettus.

Bald, with opened collar and short sleeve shirt,
facing forward as purposive as saint
or sunlight, it is eager to elucidate
but inert, so what it says sounds like this:

She sings 'bronze strigil', she sings 'clay rattle' –
the customers murmur, recovering from battle.
She lists the fish of Thessaloniki:
'Pandora, Sargo, Dentex, Bogue, Gofari.'

She sings 'an indispensible instrument
used by athletes in antiquity when
bathing after the games.' Their tiny cups
settle: it soothes away their anxious gossip.

She sings 'complete with the pebble inside,
a faithful copy of a cradle. The mattress and pillow,
very soft, sink in with the weight of the sleeping child.'
Their breathing slips away from the shallows.

She quotes the Iliad, *'Braided locks*
caught waspwise in gold and silver.'
Without needing to understand a word,
they rise, refreshed, and draw their swords.

Thersites

So he spoke and dashed the sceptre against his back and
shoulders, and he doubled over, and a round tear dropped from him,
and a bloody welt stood up between his shoulders under
the golden sceptre's stroke, and he sat down again, frightened,
in pain, and looking helplessly about wiped off the tear-drops.
Sorry though the men were they laughed over him happily…

THE ILIAD, BK 2, *ll.* 264-70

Take your paiks is every sodger's byword
jist as the arrows in their showers dinnae judge
sae our Lords cannae well distinguish
an order questioned from an order disobeyed.

I'm humphibackit cause I cannae sleep
atween my brithers in the sand aside the ships
in the close, midgie-pitchit darkness,
breathing piss and leather and our blood.

Lords dinnae curl in shattered ranks at nicht
but lie ahent their hide tents' walls
blanketed with stolen women, breast to flank,
and stare at treasures for their stars.

I hear the wounded measure hours wi groans
ignored by aa the thousands snoring in their faces,
the sentries mutter by their paced-out fires –
and every dream's the opposite of fear and blades.

Why should your dunts and curses hurt me mair,
Odysseus, although I ken you are a Lord
and a liar? Because you understand
the motion o each man's mind is separate,

and yet you order us tae be what you are not:
two souls at once: one passive as
these women you've enslaved to bicker over,
the ither vicious as the hunting dogs you kick.

You say that I'm puss-ugly when you dinnae like
my thocht; and yet my flesh is fit enough
tae fling upon a Trojan spear. How ugly
is the lie that sends a man to war?

Let the sodgers laugh the way they must,
survivors of the moments you dictate;
let them borrow your rage but inherit fear:
tomorrow is the opposite of home.

Pilgrim Street

6 *Asterion*
(for Debbie)

To have no motive makes your route a maze:
the labyrinth of such passivity
will lead you to compose the hope one phrase
may cause the lucky murk to set you free
from that deep groove each second's self can't see
the minute hand of habit helps him dig –
one phrase the dream wrote down and crammed beneath
your pillow, there to morph from babe to pig:
the memory's half-prison and half-palace
where Dedalus becomes both Minotaur and Alice.

– There has to be a paean here to Crete,
a full-on Gravesian myth-kitty scratch
for that arch-backed Psipsinna isle, complete
with recipes for history's best batch
of stone *boureki*, guides for where to watch
Gort's father, Talus, first of robots, guard
the beaches like a bronze-browed Bandersnatch –
this is the ochre turf of Epidamnus, bard
of paradox – roll down the night-cab's pane:
wild thyme and fox piss say you're home from home again.

You'll find the Hotel Labyrinthos at
that neat illegal left into Georgioupouli
which everybody takes: first, greying flats,
its random, run-down stack of balconies,
and then tavernas, mini-marts, the sea;
and where the once-malarial Almirou
still meets the bay, great eucalyptus trees
give shade to tourists wondering what to do
with all this time they've bought. Let booze and food
and sun bewilder them to sleep: the myth holds good.

Though why should Theseus fail to register
beyond a walk-on on my storyboard
of psycho-machi-allegori-core?
Is it because he has the final sword?
What is the matter with this matador
that he's so unadored, unlike Lord Byron –
both man and beast enough that none were bored
should he drop anchor in their flesh environs?
The hero simplified to butcher brings
too little to an island stocked with gods for kings.

There's Zeus or Minos or Asterion –
throw Rhadamanthus in the royal mix
of demi-goddish fathers, bullish sons –
alive: part-Pharaoh and part-Pontifex;
dead: judges in stiff session past the Styx.
Achaean Theseus whacked them obsolete
the way time pressed the archaeopteryx
beneath the pounding strata of its feet –
Crete's strange chimeric Kings were overthrown
so ordinary monsters could ascend the throne.

And then there were the women: Pasiphaë,
they fancied, hid inside a wooden cow:
beware how Greeks revise your myths as lies –
all chthonic power tamed to porn's low brow.
Though Ariadne's thread, that one true tow,
revealed their trope of labyrinth was just
a ravelled palace – rhetoric unhoused,
Nietzsche must write her how his wits were lost.
Then Gaia, giving birth, dug in her nails
creating Curetes to out-shout Zeus's wails.

Melisseus, whom Graves proclaimed a drone,
was bee-man boss of Cretan corybants –
those martial dancers Zorba would have known
but Zeus might just have got confused with ants:
Despots, or, *pace* Rob, Despinas, can't
distinguish loyal subjects from the herd –

or fear initiative in supplicants.
And Hebrew for Despina, queen of words
and bees, is Deborah – I might have known:
to serve the Goddess somehow's scrimshawed on my bone.

7 SOMALILALIA

I can't seem to fix you, quarrelsome self,
you're like that riverbed, Waaheen,
shifting between long drought, brief spate...

Your usual impact is to put
the people in two minds,
to keep them from deciding...

GAARRIYE

Flying Backwards

'Where are *you* going?' swaggered the stick,
rapped lightly against arriving ribs
till a wave from a journalist – my FT pal –
already sat at the bungalow for VIPs,
got me off the runway for some sweet red tea.

'Where are you *going*?' jollied a jellaba
back on Djibouti's runway in our brave twin-prop –
half-pencil case, half-Lada. Outside,
the seats were being removed from its comrade
so sheep could board, then promenade.

'Hargeisa, insha'Allah' prayed its pilot
and a glance behind caught the engineer a-
kimbo on our luggage with a shaky thumbs up.
An hour of glassy scrub, then two rocky cones:
'See there? – the titties of Hargeisa!'

'Where *are* you going?' the hijab had hummed
on the flight out from Heathrow, a tiny mother
perched upon a bale of cloth for others –
and when the answer widened those eyes:
'Are you a journalist?' – I had no reply.

She could, by a dextrous twist upon
the necessary hour, pray in her seat
while I anticipated everybody's question
as though my insides knew.
Where was she heading? 'Home to Mogadishu.'

'*Where* are you going?' tasked a telephone,
its actuary eagerness to sell upon
the wane, then told my ear the same
re a former colony as the FO:
'Somaliland? – No coverage for there.'

News from Hargeisa

Somali Bedouins have a passion for knowing how the world wags...
news flies through the country. Among the wild Gudabirsi the Russian
war was a topic of interest, and at Harar I heard of a violent storm,
which had damaged the shipping in Bombay Harbour, but a few weeks
after the event.

RICHARD BURTON, First Footsteps in East Africa

1

First thing: a simcard from the tower of TeleSom,
that meant – anywhere – I could call home,
including the desert's heart, Laas Geel,
where my mother called to ask if I was ill (I was).

No: first first thing, Gaarriye in a 4x4
straight through security – papers and chains a bore –
the poem's a Somali open sesame; then home
past grand hotels, slabbed off from car-bombs

that never came; qat booths and the dry-throat river;
past shops named after him – purveyors
of electronics, fridges; the Brit-built parliament,
decayed and delaying; the new Obama Restaurant.

We sped through everything, punctual as news or qat
itself, to a little backyard, its allotted slot of stars.

2

Beneath his lime-green eaves in the white-tiled strip
of courtyard, carpeted to make a bedroom,
I stare at the stars as Gaarriye points out Gurey
like a square sky-robot, tiny-headed hero,
doomed offspring of a murderous she-djinn –
his only choice was matricide. Is this how to begin
in Hargeisa – my hotel room unslept-in,
frozen in the comet-tails of conversation,
stories for the lines that link the stars?

151

Between soft pancake mornings of fresh papaya, clove tea,
and smoky kitchen evenings of Somali classes,
(*kuluyl* is heat and *qiiq* is smoke), the grammar of samosas
(*macaan* is delicious); the night sky become a visor
through which the Moon stares down on our sleeping faces –
we begin to live inside air's letterbox, outside
the women's way with folding, wiping, frying, words,
that lifts the children through their courtyard years:
stories as the lines that link their stars.

3

The hyena and the lion shared a kill
and the lion, as befits a king, said, 'Split
the carcass and the innards and the bones
between us so we both may dine.'
The hyena gave the lion nine-tenths
of the poor gazelle and grabbed the rest –
his king roared out, 'What's this?' and raked
the creature with its claw-stuck club
of a paw so hard an eyeball hung
like white fruit on the smirker's cheek.

A fox came trotting from the darkness:
'Let me see the portion that he took –
why, you should have nine-tenths of this!'
and so divided it, and then, before
the lion spoke, said, 'Still, a king must have
nine-tenths of what remains...' and so,
though it was only cartilage and gut,
divided it once more, and then again,
until the lion had its share, and let
the fox and all his kinsmen live.

4

Gaarriye checking Al-Jazeera daily for the latest
in the hot curtain-drawn long low-sofa sitting room
re the US captain bobbing in his Hitchcock lifeboat
off Puntland with three doomed pirates

did they but know it, while I note down parables
and chafe to see the MiG parked by Gobannimo Market
where Siyaad Barre strafed his own citizens
and we buy mp3s of oud music, ounces of frankincense –

which Mas'ūdī mentions in *The Meadows of Gold*
as the whole coast's only ancient export – *kundur*,
great scoops of its heady grey gum for a few wads
of shillings; swathes of *shammaad*, women's cloth,

patterns like shadows scissoring bougainvillea,
for which Gaarriye reckons he can get me a deal.
Back home past exposed cellars and piled breezeblocks:
a massive new build they simply call 'MI6'.

5

There is a tree upon the moon
a sparse old country much like ours
whose each leaf mirrors one of us
and when we're born it's glad and green
and as we grow it burns to gold
and when we sicken it turns white
and when we're dying then it drops
falling for forty days and nights
and no one knows which is the cause
and which is the effect, but when
it touches for the first time here
and curls up, as it dries we die.

6

We slept so close
to the silent pool of sky
that when the baby cried
it was as though the moon
wept papaya-coloured light

as though it could believe
the galaxies infect us with music

153

like Gaarriye's toothache groans,
till all our infant languages
learn to praise the night

so while we slept
and the blue dogs curled in the road
Hargeisa's dry stars knelt
and kissed our brows
with insects for their lips.

Earth-pig

Dutch colonists gave it its name, which means 'earth pig', because it resembles in some respects the pig and because of the amazing efficiency with which it can burrow into the ground, notably to create the system of tunnels in which it lives.
ALAN DAVIDSON, The Oxford Companion to Food

Asleep upon the only road to Ethiopia
like a sow my father had tickled down its vertebrae,
we had to stop the convoy to inspect it,
our guard trailing his AK's stock across the grit.

An aardvaark on a two-lane highway,
the desert exhaling the promise of rain
into its drawn-back lips, its long grey snout,
columns of termites drawing near to look.

I wanted its claws, still dirty with the darkness
underground, to twitch; I wanted to taste
with that tongue, protruding as though it wrote
a difficult sentence on the shell-pocked road.

I wanted to read the whole road with that pointer
as though it were an unscrolled tape, an epic
of tar, stuck with every voice, on which was lain,
like a grey uncoiling comma, the earth-pig.

The Captives

Termite mounds step closer when your head turns,
towers that seem the opposite of edifice –
not constructed from below but as though
remains of some eroded solid, anterior to air,
the megalopolis that once gripped us all –

the way that Bete Giyorgis, that church in Lalibela,
sits within the pit, as though it dreamed itself
while still inside the rock they carved it from;
or Pompeii's smothered souls had found their feet,
zombie husks, shufflers by the roadsides,

frozen when you look, both fecal and phallic,
still enshrouded in sackcloth, still bonded –
a burqa of earth obscures their nearly faces,
they haul and lean in exhaustion, herd the unseen,
cloud shadows hint at their caprines, *riyo* or *ido*

ready to scatter in this rainy season; but
they pause, burdened by the cities within them
in a cityless place, their nerve tunnels, legions
of blind thoughts grubbing away, irrigating breath
through breathlessness, they anxiously approach

as though they have requests, questions about
release, curiosities that we could feed
but when we turn they will not speak,
these captives wandered far from some tomb
they should have been immured within,

from the rock that would have folded them
in its embrace, its chain that fused, the mouths
that should have been inscribed, the hand
that could have held, the chisel dropped away
and all the termite text escaping into earth

Riyo: goats; *ido:* sheep.

156

Hotel Rays

1

Hospitium enclosus: a wiry light cloisonnés the lawn
upon which, ambassador of grass, the tortoise lives –
slow lawnmower, cracked and shifting whaleback
in its square Sargasso, solemn gazer on
the kudu, streak-flanked as though it had just leaned
against a freshly-painted zebra. Neither may leave.

We breakfasted on liver and mango,
hardly mentioning the aid worker, shot
four years ago, but got the shivers when,
Gaarriye-less, the guard would not let us past
to climb a hillside that wanted to be a lane
through children playing, free as feathers.

2

After we'd read to the usual three hundred
in a hall for half that in the old boarding school
they'd declared Amoud University – plus a stunned row
of just-arrived Americans, tutors: suncreamed, headscarfed
and wholly unready for 'the fine ear of these people' –

Riyaale, wry Dean of Student Affairs, drove us up
to Old Amoud: a slave station en route to the Red Sea;
a territory he described as 'God's land', meaning
no one wanted to live there. Startling what must be
Phillip's dik-diks, darting from our flanks, we rose to rubble.

The city wall straggled at two courses; then strewn pottery,
pure quartz, sockets of fire-blackened millet stores –
sucking out the air with flame will keep the grain
for twenty years – just twenty years before he'd seen
walls up to the window-frames and the old chains.

'Brokers,' he said, looking down at Boorama's bowl
where colonials had hunted lion. 'We were brokers.'
We went back by a half-built hospital, stairwell
blocked with Saudi carpets. Broken, still mirrored
in a name, memory negotiates the cure or the kill.

3

The hotel's name, Rays, means the lying of fresh rain
on the ground, so, while yellow weaver birds,
possibly Speke's, plait their lunch-song
(*chinkichi-chewchew-skerinkitistew*),

and Martin and I discuss how in a poem
a conversation between a lover and a crow
can be like a camel with a peg through its nose
so it can't smell the calf it feeds,

suddenly, gently, then with great, dark-
spotted insistence, it begins to rain,
so fresh a smell it is as though
the air is being rinsed clean of song.

4

Before dusk could lean on the whole continent
another of Amoud's thirty-year-old Deans,
Axmed, took us out to the airport, to watch a herd
of goats taxi down its long dust runway,
and Martin persuaded the herder to sing a *hees*.

She giggled at our desire to hear goat-music as
the sun took off, and her black and white charges
turned grey as she swished sticks and sang to them
and the stone-curlews, the one flightless transporter
and the broad valley, asphalt-free to its hills.

Some boys were summoned by her song
arriving like the Constellation of the Haggler
to establish a rate for this. Axmed's advice –
nothing so generous as to cause
dispute between cousins over a voice.

5

And then the cry comes up and the cry comes up
from another and the cry comes up from
another and another mosque

the comfort of the calls to prayer
itself a kind of reply as they arise
almost at the same moment

on all sides around the little hilltop
of Buurta Sheekh Cali, up from the dark
and into the not yet dark

as though the delay was caused by darkness
itself, gathering around our prayers
as the kids play on the timbers stacked

below the mobile phone mast and the Sufi shrine
and pose for photos as this hill's last mosque sings out
a few lights are lit and the smell of woodsmoke rises

and as two girls run down the almost sheer slope in
their flip-flops and a mother in her patchwork hut
calls suddenly for flour and before

we descend to buy batteries and *caday*,
new bundles of toothbrush twigs on a streetcorner,
the cries continue ascending into the darker still,

rising to where everything is
still, where prayer will only consent to be heard
beyond the human ear

Saxansaxo (Driving Westward)

And being by others hurried every day,
Scarce in a year their natural form obey...
DONNE

Hours after the professoriate
have packed their cases, having chewed their qat,
it's time to be trying to race the rain
westward and home to Hargeisa.

Past the burnt-out tanks by Bad Luck Farm,
beside the tarmac if the track goes faster
like the arrowing swift, the *baaqfallaar*,
the driver keeps a nostril to the onrushing cloud.

We chafe at hamlets with a chain across
shell-pocked asphalt, guard-sheds from which
men amble to slap the poet's happy hand
and shout hello to us, *xerta* of alliteration's sheekh.

A Y-shaped treestump burns in the darkened
rain-stalked desert. When Gaarriye flings
a qat branch from the window it flies back
and slaps his brow like angry laurels.

Now even I inhale it, where the hills
are scoured back to a few scant pyramids,
between grit-blown trees that graft beside
the sere and sandy riverbeds: *saxansaxo*,

sweet scent of approaching rain
that means split wrist-bone beds of sunken rivers
will spate with an express engineered from water
and we must crowd at their crossings for hours.

As we hurry, half-reluctant, before rain's arrival,
I stare into a dream of streaming carriages
passengers nose-deep in the pulse of news:
Mas'ūdī and Burton, the imam John Donne.

Laas Geel

Glister and grit of the semiprecious desert
crinkle-paned quartz and rumour of ruby
perpetually blink at the bobbing edge
of vision, that circle we're always verging upon
approaching the scorched terracotta outcrops

great gourd-shapes of rock dropped as though
thigh-deep into the pulsing plain, rounded
as groundnut casings in the glaze of noon
and wormed with open caves, found thrones
and readymade council rooms from which a court

of monkeys has recently absconded, leaving us
to their inheritance of galleries, murals
of the cattle people, vanished from hereabouts
like the grasslands where their painted herds,
these tent-like walls of flesh, would graze.

Ochre echoes follow every bump and hollow,
knowingly as lovers' fingers show
cattle flat as flags that graze the ghosts
of pasture past which haunt this herdless gulch,
beasts vaster than the spreading hands

of little T-shaped men – us, but set below, behind:
arms attempting to embrace this same horizon
as though they can't believe all things are still free,
their Africa ample as a broody beast, and ours
the horns and bones and walking skins of shadow.

Berbera

But I was telling how I was inspired to visit Cilmi's grave,
To offer my homage, my salutations and my song...
HADRAAWI

What lasts and what do we want to last
if memory's made new by thinking it again,
a fable finding its latest mouth each time
and lost beyond your final thought? Not

the drive to Berbera – a race with freshness,
since the day's catch would not be served
a moment later than, like everything Somali,
its optimum. So we blurred past the site

where a friend of Martin's father won his VC,
holding a hill with a handful of men
like the veterans we'd met at the NGO, still in
their scoutish uniforms, hair red with henna.

They stopped the Italian advance across
a border now as invisible to all
former and would-be future masters as
those medalled men, or this self-declared

republic, still fitting within its limits.
We dropped from the hills into coastal heat
like an undercarriage skidding on the runway
ahead, the only one long enough, they say,

to land the Shuttle outside of Houston. Not
the good smell, *udgoon*, of fried fish, *kalluun*,
in the salt and dusty haze past noon and by the Gulf,
tray-fulls in the guestless hotel, malt non-beer.

Not the swim, each breaker lifting its swirl of sand
into sunlight, the guards, lounging on cardboard,
no older than those boys who rushed into the surf
to help the diver drag his boat ashore – a Brit,

head filled with brilliant fingers of unbroken coral,
the unrecorded paths of migrating whales:
I was the nearest he could find to a tourist
so got to hear his perfect pitch.

Not the drive back into dusk and doubt,
talk of walking in the green pastures, *doog*,
as we reached white sand, mountains streaked
with black lava: *guban* and darkness where

I keep seeing lightning across the bush
no one else notices – rain somewhere other,
light's brief inhabiting of air, a striplight
attached to the flat cloud-ceiling that flickers.

Not that, neither our coming nor going,
but the search for the baker's grave,
Cilmi Bowndheri, who Hadraawi greeted
as his 'king among poets', Hodon's lover.

We found only a broken length, nameless,
collapsing back into powdery dirt,
no cemetery wall, no limit to its fading,
no end to the final act of his forgetting.

The Lamb

I hadn't been aware, although I'd watch
as his friends made that flicking gesture
at their throats, of the steady approach
of the liver for our final feast, borne
within the black-headed sheep
like a Sheban queen within her litter,

a Berbera blackhead selected by
Gaarriye's half-brother out past Gebiley
and driven here since our arrival
by steady switchings with his crook
like a Neapolitan's stroking of his cheek
sketching the scar of the hard man

I was not: some bug had stopped me
as though in the whole herd's tracks
so I missed reading with Hadraawi
in a hall I wandered later, looking through
the hot absence of seven hundred people
for a poem blown beneath the chairs

by the poets' breath – still shaky, with
no appetite, as though I were the paper.
So when a neighbour, in whose yard
the sheep had spent its first enclosured night,
handed me her well-honed, hair-thin knife
I couldn't amount to the honour,

and she, practical and brief, cut through
its butter neck where black head becomes
white throat, as though God's guidance,
almost severing it with that stroke,
and sent arterial plumes to pelt the wall,
and felled it in the little courtyard.

Gaarriye's youngest daughter laughed to see
its silly fall, but wept as lid and container
of those few years of grazing and sun's grace
continued to think they could be alive
as though there were some catch, some pin
that thrashing would rebutton up.

And then, instead of life, its echo:
the pipes within it sounding out their last,
and like an offering to summon ghosts,
the deep bowl blood made for itself
by gouging into dust, as the carcass
was seized and hung upon the porch.

And then I saw how the flies were gathered
like a shadow thrown into the air
by the sharp unlacing of the stomach wall,
presence of the viscera another visitor
as the liver, like a newborn lamb, was lifted
and we gathered for the feast.

Pilgrim Street

7 *Daedalics*

We're filled, the muses claim, with tripes and tropes –
among their ticks and scrawny-throated herds,
they perch upon their high, pine-stubbled slopes
and don't know how to tell us we diverge:
our bags of guts and bowls of words each surge
in contrary directions. Poor old flesh –
muscle, corpuscle, nerve – can only lurch
to burial, while neuron will enmesh
with neuron, till our consciousness constructs
a mind, which burrows birth-wards, claiming to induct.

Paideuma – that tangling of the roots by which,
Frobenius whispered in Pound's Greekish ear,
we apprehend how children of the rich
think they own history. Not that he could hear
for looking like a Sinologic seer,
nor could he see through Fenellosa's flaw:
the Chinese do not read the pictures, dear.
Confusion cooked his book and called it raw.
And parataxis is not ideogrammic,
unless it's truth with which you're being economic.

But every Dedalus forgets in turn
his home key through the practice of his art,
departs from Fibonacci when he learns
the goal was only useful as a start:
to build the labyrinth he must lose heart,
lose head, lose compass, hand and face –
let instinct tear his faculties apart:
the Minotaur can't know it's in a maze –
one whisper and his true creation's lost.
And so he haunts his life as though half-beast, half-ghost.

At forty-nine, Dunce Scotus Gyrovagus,
why still attempt books doubled as the labrys,
too troubled to read half of, thrown away as
OCD-meets-whim? Formally too barbarous
to draw the scholars to their proper libraries;
too full of hohos for the hoitytoit –
no one eternal note with candelabras;
too shirty and too shouty, too 'not quite' –
no hero, then, no Theseus, no Childe,
some porter gone to seed, his Walls of Troy grown wild.

Why did you, Dustie-Fute, compose in Scots –
a language no one's taught they need to read,
that's filled with forty synonyms for snot
and spoken mainly by the rural deid?
Our word for 'language', laughably, is 'leid' –
that's less the vanguard, more the zeppelin
which plummets from the 'lift' *qua* 'sky'. Who needs
to learn another English for their sins?
How many angels would it take, if Lallans
could skriek, or jist creh oot their names, to shift this balance?

What drove you to translate the lesser-known
rest of the world – Chinese, Somali, Turkish,
Bulgarian and Farsi? Chance alone,
or (this rhyme only works upon the ticklish)
some instinct that you must become unRilkeish?
Beyond the Eurodome it's audible
how Byron found a global sort of Unglish
that tells an angel from the ego's yell,
finds muses up muezzins, orreries
in Mandarin, and in Cyrillic how to sneeze.

And how on earth or on the moon to finish
this travelogue of the unravelling voice
which can't go home again? Say we just vanish
in a Cortina – neither Rolls nor Royce
would understand the weird behind that choice –

let's go. The essence is an excellence
at running, said auld Dedalus as Joyce:
beyond the gut-mind and the roar of sense
in Hotel Labyrinthos monsters greet:
the Silk Road and the Low Road meet on Pilgrim Street.

Epode

'Same again,' you ask at The Dog and Barrel,
and its Heraclitean barman replies,
'How can you have the same again?'
Please check your change or, in the Greek, *ta resta*:
could it cool an eyelid? Is it good enough to eat?
Study the ice in your glass for clues
as to its origins or yours –

the way you look through the ripples in your face
reflected in Not-the-Same River, and notice
is your second toe not longer on the right?
Praxiteles wouldn't lift his chisel for you,
nor Pindar consider a loser's ode.

Meanwhile your mind persists in its asymmetries
like two old foes who're forced to try
each other's lyrics on instead of armour.
All your scars are down the clumsy side
which is probably what has brought your body here
to the man-eating river.

In the corner not the apple of your eye
translucent as a floating cell or shrimp,
an infant's ankle hangs above the brim:
the iceberg of the rest of grim Achilles
has melted in your myths' arterial flow.

You almost see the indent of his mother's thumb
printless as the gods remain, and understand,
for once, the change you can't believe in
has come upon you, both suddenly and at last.

And here is where the muses now dictate
I must explain by 'you' they mean the species,
mere bags of lies and flies and innards,

all crowding in the foetal shallows,
clinging to the facts like flesh to bones.
This is the River Styx. Your name is No Man
and you have fought well, indifferently, or not at all.

This is the River Lethe, and your boat
is departing now, except there is no boat.
Cabinned crew will splash among you with
your complementary flute-full of Omnesia.
This is the River Jordan and, although
there is milk and honey, there is no other side.
This is the change that is, forever,
as good as a rest. This is the river.

ACKNOWLEDGEMENTS

'The Messages' was commissioned by the sculptor David Annand to be inscribed on a piece, 'Cubes', for Tesco's in Dundee. 'The Silver Bridie' appeared on *North Carr Light*. 'Rabbie, Rabbie, Burning Bright' and 'Cock of the North' appeared in *New Poems Chiefly in the Scottish Dialect*, ed. Robert Crawford (Polygon, 2009). 'End-Sang' was commissioned for *Headshook*, ed. Stuart Kelly (Hachette Scotland, 2009). 'An Epistle' was commissioned for *Addressing the Bard*, ed. Douglas Gifford (Scottish Poetry Library, 2009). The sequence *Muqam* appeared on *Mad Hatters Review*. 'Thersites', the sequence *A Myth of Scotland*, and 'Epode' were variously commissioned by BBC Radios 3 and 4. 'The Whale Road' was a collaboration with the artist Christine Kelegher for *Hidden Door*. 'The Library of Bronze' appeared in *Split Screen* (Red Squirrel Press, 2012).

Poems also appeared in *Almost Island, And Other Poems, Blackbox Manifold, Chapman, Edinburgh Review, Gift, The Guardian, Ink Sweat and Tears, Magma, Poetry International Web, Poetry London, Poetry Scotland, Poetry Wales, The Warwick Review* and *The White Review*.

I would like to thank the British Council, Cove Park, and the organisers of the Pamirs, Guangzhou, Poeteka, Venezuelan World Poetry and Druskininkai Festivals, for the stimulus behind many of these poems. Thanks also to Martin Orwin for his help and kindness re all matters Somali. I would also like to thank Linda Anderson and Jenny Richards, and my colleagues at the School of English Literature Language and Linguistics, Newcastle University, for all their support during the composition and completion of *Omnesia*.